EARLY PRAISE FOR
FROM THE GROUND UP

"Wow! This book is here; we've needed it for so long. The truth of our dynamic, powerful, practical, passionate potential for impact has been suppressed, yet it is accessible. Christy lights the path for us. Let's save democracy!" —Angie Smith

"This book sheds light on the importance of women's representation in local and state elections (many of which have uncontested seats). Christy provides a roadmap for how to get involved and solid verification for why we should do so, explaining that even if you feel you are not ready, most women are well prepared for these leadership roles due to the everyday things we do in life: caring for families, running our households, and advocating for things we feel are important in our communities. This book reads like a well-written motivational speech that will get you ready to jump into action." —Debra Blue

"There is a moment in time amidst the chaos of the macro bullhorn of politics when truth, inspiration, and action synchronize together in one subtle swoop that leaves you decisively inspired! The storyline makes the case and shows insight into the wins you already hold and how to use that momentum to run for public office. The author's research and perspective thoughtfully lay out the red carpet to your win!" —Diana Maldonado

"I am forever changed by this book. This book makes me feel seen and heard, and helps me to see and hear others...all while reinforcing the quiet (and sometimes not-so-quiet) ideas in my head, heart, and soul. If you feel like you have reached critical mass in these crazy days, this book is your tipping point to claim your place in creating a more peaceful and functional world. Thank you, Christy Jaynes, for guiding us to our voices, our courage, and possibly, our purpose." — Betsy Davis

"A must-read for every woman who cares about her country! Christy has thoughtfully laid out a clear, actionable game plan to create, design, and execute meaningful change in government. She sparks hope and determination, making this book an empowering call to action for female citizens ready to step up and make a difference." —Meg Hays

"Smashing through the political overwhelm! Christy makes it clear just how we can show up in ALL the ways that support meaningful change. And it isn't as daunting as we probably all might think. Advocate and support where you are, and change will come. Heroes can come from the quietest corners of society." —Sandy Stewart

"Pissed off? Angry? Frightened about the future? Take an hour off from scrolling and start reading this book. You'll know what to do about it. So sensible, wise, and specific, this book may inspire the next big change in your life and in your community's." —Marsha Smellkinson

"If you've had it up to here with the state of the world, or just the state of the world you live in, and wondered what you can do about it, here's the solution you've been looking for. Christy Jaynes makes a passionate case for why more women should be running for office, and not just any office: local politics. Equal parts pep talk and manifesto, this book will help fan that fire you've been itching to start. Whether you've felt the call, or just the frustration, consider this your invitation to step in and start making change where it matters most—close to home!" —Kristi Koeter

"Even as a mature woman, there are times I think, 'hmmm, why didn't I know this already?' Today was one of those days. Christy's book provides a stepping off point for people just like me, and you, and everyone in between. By the end of chapter one, I was ready to make my voice heard; to stand up and take action in MY community. If you find yourself depressed about the state of our country but think you don't have a voice to change it, think again and then run to buy this book! If not for yourself, for another strong woman who doesn't yet know she already has what it takes - desire to do better."

—Jennifer Dickerson

WOMEN LIKE YOU ARE SAVING DEMOCRACY, HERE'S HOW:

FROM THE GROUND UP

Christy Jaynes

Fin PRESS

FinPressBooks.com

Copyright © 2025 by Christy Jaynes and Fin Press Books

All rights reserved.

No part of this publication may be reproduced, distributed, or transmitted in any form or by any means, electronic, mechanical, photocopying, recording, or otherwise, without the prior written permission of the publisher, except in the case of brief quotations used in critical reviews or articles, except as permitted by U.S. copyright law.

Paperback: 979-8-9930839-0-2

Ebook: 979-8-9930839-3-3

Edited by Alyssa Rabil

Interior Design Nicolette Halladay

First Edition, 2025

Printed in the United States of America

For permission requests, write to the publisher at:

Fin Press Books

https://www.finpressbooks.com

For Diana, you carry the torch that lit my political fire.

CONTENTS

Introduction xi

1. When Icy Hearts Rule The World, Set it On Fire 1
2. Leadership Looks Like You 11
3. The Local Roots of National Change: 17
   This Is What Power Looks Like
4. What the Hell Am I Even Running For? 29
5. How to Actually Get on the Ballot 35
6. You Can't Shame a Woman Who's Already Done the Work 41
7. The Politics of Becoming Her 47
8. Victory is Just The Beginning 53
9. You've Won, No Matter How The Race is Called 63
10. Life, and Life After Office 67

Afterword 73
How will we know if any of this makes a real difference?

Part Two 77

LET'S GET TO WORK

You Said Yes?! 87
Campaign Starter Kit 91
Glossary of Campaign Terms 105
Index of Works Cited 117
About the Author 119

INTRODUCTION
YOU, ME, AND THE AMERICAN FUTURE

Let me set the scene.

You're standing in the checkout line, scrolling headlines, trying not to scream. Another policy passed that makes no sense. Another leader saying things so detached from reality you wonder if it's satire. Another person in power using it like a weapon. You put your phone down, grip the cart handle a little harder, and think to yourself:

Somebody needs to fix this.

And maybe, just maybe-some some small, irreverent, revolutionary voice inside you whispers:

What if that somebody is me?

If that voice has ever visited you, at the school board meeting, during a kitchen-table rant, or while rage-folding laundry, then this book is for you.

You don't need to already see yourself as a politician. In fact, I hope you don't. Because the truth is, we've had enough politicians.

Introduction

I wasn't always politically engaged. For years, I voted, but I stayed quiet online, avoided tense family conversations, and kept politics at a distance. I told myself it was too messy, too angry, too complicated. But a couple of years ago, I began working on a project to guide women who wanted to run for office. And the deeper I went, the more I realized: I couldn't unsee what I had seen. There are golden opportunities all around us, hidden in city councils, school boards, local commissions, places where women can make history. But most people don't even know those doors are open. The morning after the 2024 election, I rolled over in bed, looked at my phone, and wept. It wasn't just sadness, it was bone-deep grief. I felt the cracking of something sacred, the unraveling of a country that won't ever be the same. And I knew I couldn't sit still. This book is my response. It's my offering. My form of activism. People often ask me why I don't run for office myself, and the truth is, I'm an advocate through and through. My superpower is helping women rise into positions of power, and that's where you come in.

What we need now are leaders.

Smart, compassionate, grounded, fire-hearted women who understand real life because they've lived it. Women who are tired of watching decisions get made by people who seem more committed to maintaining power than serving people. Women who want to build, not just criticize.

I'm not here to sell you a dream.

I'm here to hand you the map. Because somewhere between "I'm furious" and "I'm filing" is a path for you. And no, it doesn't require perfection, pedigree, or permission. But I know what stands in the way. I know what it feels like to lie awake at night scrolling through terrible news, fighting off that hollow ache in your chest, the one that asks, Is any of this even fixable? The grief you carry isn't just about politics. It's about the fear that something sacred is slipping away. That cruelty is spreading faster than

Introduction

compassion. That the country you were taught to believe in might not love you back. And in that heaviness, it's easy to go numb. To ask, Who will fix this? Who will save us? How am I supposed to get out of bed, raise kids, go to work, pay bills, show up for people, and still have the energy to fight for a better future?

You don't ask those questions because you're weak. You ask them because you care. Because you see what's happening. And, because you haven't given up hope, not really. Not yet. And maybe that flicker of hope, fragile as it feels, is the bravest thing about you. Because even in the middle of your exhaustion, something in you is still whispering, We can do better. Even as the weight of it all pushes down, you still get up. You still show up for your people. You still sign the petition. You still speak up in the meeting. You still make dinner, pay rent, offer kindness, and carry the story forward. And that, that persistence? That's political. That's sacred. That's the heartbeat of this entire country.

So, no, you don't need to be fearless to run.

You just need to be willing to take the next right step, even with your voice shaking.

You don't need to save the whole country.

You just need to claim your corner of it and say, Not on my watch.

You don't need to be unbreakable.

You just need to be honest, open, and ready to remember that power doesn't belong to the few. It belongs to us. To the many, if we're willing to reach for it. And the fact that you're still here, still reading, still feeling– that means you're already on your way.

You might be a teacher. A parent. A nurse. A bartender. A woman with opinions and a spine and a vision for how things could be better. You might not feel ready, but most of the people running things right now weren't either. They just said yes.

This book is your yes. Or maybe, your maybe.

Introduction

It's your invitation to step into public life without losing your private self. To run for something without running yourself into the ground. To lead with both grit and grace, and maybe a good swear word or two.

And yes, this is momentous.

Every time a woman steps into public power without contorting herself to fit the mold, she cracks the mold a little more. Every time she governs with empathy and holds the line on justice, she teaches her community what leadership really looks like. Every time she runs, not away, but toward, she pulls history with her.

We're not just asking for a seat at the table anymore. We're reshaping the table itself, where every voice counts, every perspective is valued, and every decision moves us closer to real win-win outcomes.

So come with me. Not because you're sure. Not because you have it all figured out. Come because something in you knows it's time.

History is calling.

And she sounds a lot like you.

1

WHEN ICY HEARTS RULE THE WORLD, SET IT ON FIRE

"This is now. Now is, all there is. Don't wait for then, strike the spark light the fire."
— Rumi

*L*et's just say it out loud: **The government is contradicting itself every damn day.**

Monday, it promises freedom.

Tuesday, it bans a book.

Wednesday, it votes to "protect children", and on Thursday, it defunds their schools, guts their healthcare, and calls it fiscal responsibility.

We are told to trust the process.

But what happens when the process is rigged to protect power, not people?

When the same lawmakers who preach about family values

ignore the thousands of families living in poverty under the policies *they* passed?

This isn't just hypocrisy. It's a full-blown identity crisis in motion, and the country's wearing a mask so tight, it can't even hear itself screaming anymore.

And where's the outrage?

Where's the uprising?

We've got pockets of it, yes, moments of brilliance and backbone.

But where's the collective thunder?

I'll tell you where: buried under propaganda, arrogance, and apathy.

That's the machine. It's designed to exhaust you.

To make politics feel like a toxic mess you're better off ignoring.

To split us into teams so busy hating each other, we forget to look up and ask, *who's writing the rules?*

But here's the thing.

You picked up this book.

You are not among the apathetic.

You might be tired. You might be overwhelmed. You might be grieving, seething, or just plain confused. But you are *not* asleep.

Because somewhere in you is a hum. A signal. A sharp little whisper that says: *Something's wrong. Something must be done. And maybe, just maybe, I'm the one to do it.*

That whisper? That's your beginning.

Because when you look around right now, with clear eyes and an honest heart, it's hard not to see it: **Everything feels broken.** The systems. The leadership. The logic. The way billionaires can buy a social media platform before single moms can afford prenatal care. The way we celebrate "historic" representation in Congress while school boards are banning books and voting rights are hanging by a thread.

You feel it, right?

That hot rage humming just beneath the surface?

That bone-deep knowing that this country could be *so much more* if we just had people—**women**—in power who actually give a damn?

You're not imagining it. You're not being dramatic. You're witnessing a nation in need of a course correction, and *you're not alone in wanting to be part of it.*

You're awake.

And being awake in this country right now is both a blessing and a burden. It means you see the cracks. But it also means you're one of the people who can do something about them. This book is your permission slip and your battle cry.

Let's bust one of the biggest lies Americans have been sold: That your only job as a citizen is to vote every four years in the presidential election and hope for the best. That's the myth of the every-four-years fix.

Nope. That's not how change works.

That's how *distraction* works.

Because while everyone's eyes are glued to the drama of presidential campaigns, there are local and state elections happening **every single year**, quietly, consistently, and with far more influence over your day-to-day life.

Your trash pickup schedule?

Local.

Your kid's curriculum?

Local.

Whether your landlord gets regulated or your neighborhood gets sidewalks?

Yep—local.

And across the country, there are **over 500,000 elected offices** below the federal level. City councils. School boards. Water districts. County commissions. Sheriffs. Judges. State legislators. Zoning boards. Transit authorities. Election clerks. The list goes on.

Most people don't even know these positions exist. And because of that, here's what happens:

Thousands of these seats go uncontested. Every. Single. Year.

That means one guy, who's been in the role for fifteen years and maybe shows up, maybe doesn't, just keeps winning. Not because he's great. But because **no one else runs.**

In some districts, *no one even files* to run.

The seat stays empty. The power goes unused.

The community gets neglected, and no one is held to account.

It's not just unfortunate. It's a missed opportunity the size of a freight train.

While people scream about broken systems from the sidelines, the systems stay broken, because the rooms where decisions get made are half-empty, and the ballots are thinner than they should be.

Here's the good news: that also means **there's room for you.**

Many of these positions are part-time. Some don't even require a campaign. A few flyers, a few coffee chats, and a few dozen votes might be all it takes. And in return? You get real power. To change budgets. Shift priorities. Protect communities. Set the tone for what's fair and what's possible.

So, yes, vote in the presidential election.

But know this: that vote is not the finish line, it's the **starting gate**.

The real action is happening closer to home, year after year, seat after seat.

And a lot of those seats?

They're still wide open.

And they're waiting for someone like you.

You might be thinking: "Politics? Me? That sounds exhausting."

Or messy. Or intimidating. Or like something other people do, people with law degrees, last names on buildings, or a weird appetite for public humiliation. But politics isn't just for the polished and the power-hungry. Politics is for people who give a damn.

It's for the woman who's tired of screaming into the void.

For the mom who can't get her kid a therapist because the waitlist is eight months long.

For the daughter who watched her dad work a full-time job and still ration insulin.

It's for the teacher, the server, the social worker, the artist.

It's for the woman who never thought she was "political" but suddenly finds herself cursing at school board livestreams and wondering who the hell is making these decisions. Spoiler: a lot of the time, it's men with bad track records and a startling lack of vision. And here's the kicker, most of them aren't any more qualified than you. They just said yes.

And that's what I'm asking you to consider now. Not a campaign plan. Not a five-year strategy.

Just a yes.

Yes to entertaining the possibility that maybe the voice you've spent your whole life refining, through motherhood, heartbreak, activism, caregiving, building businesses, surviving, dreaming, wasn't just for storytelling over wine.

Maybe it's for shaping your city.

Your state.

Your slice of this country.

We've been fed a cartoon version of leadership. Stiff suits. Hollow speeches. The same five names on repeat since 1987.

But real leadership? It looks like the woman who walks into the DMV with snacks for the staff because she knows how hard their jobs are. It looks like the grandma who raised half the neighborhood and still shows up to every town hall.

It looks like *you*, tired but lit up, pissed but hopeful, showing up again because something in you refuses to go numb.

Civic leadership doesn't require perfection; it requires proximity. It's not about knowing every policy detail. It's about knowing your people, and being willing to fight for them, visibly and out loud.

And then there's the line we've all heard, maybe even said ourselves:

"I'm not political."

"I stay out of all that."

"It's too toxic. Too overwhelming. Not for me."

Let's talk about what that really means.

Because if you've ever said those words, here's what you're *actually* saying, whether you realize it or not:

"I don't feel safe. I don't feel powerful. I don't think my voice will make a difference."

And let me tell you: That's not apathy. That's grief.

Grief for a country that's made politics feel like a rich man's game.

Grief for the decades where our power was mocked, ignored, legislated against.

Grief for how *exhausting* it is to survive in a system that rarely sees your full humanity.

So when a woman says she's not political, I don't judge her.

But I *do* want her to know the cost of staying on the sidelines.

Politics isn't just something that happens on CNN. It's not just shouting on the floor of Congress or slick attack ads during election season.

I was talking to a man just after the last presidential election, apathetic, frustrated, the way so many people feel when they believe the system's broken beyond repair. I asked him what mattered to him, what he wanted to see change. He rattled off a list.

Housing costs. School quality. Police accountability. Roads that never got fixed.

Every single item? A local or state issue. Not one of them was something the President alone could change. But he didn't know that. He didn't even realize who was making the rules or how to reach them.

And that's the problem.

We're fed this idea that change only happens at the top, so we tune out everything else. But real life? Real problems? They get solved, or ignored, closer to home. That's why we have to look up from our phones, learn who holds the power in our communities, and study the issues at their source.

Before we point a finger, we have to know where to point it.

Before we can fix anything, we have to understand what's broken, and who's benefitting from keeping it that way.

Politics is whether your neighborhood has sidewalks. Whether your kid's school has clean water. Whether your friend gets to vote without jumping through hoops.

It's whether your mom's prescription is affordable. Whether your sister can get childcare. Whether your best friend can marry the person she loves and be protected under the law.

Politics is everywhere. It's everything.

And when you "stay out of it," you don't escape the system, you stop shaping it. You give your voice to the loudest, not the wisest. You give your future to people who may not have your best interest at heart.

But here's the real kicker: *You don't have to know everything to begin.* You don't need a degree in policy. You don't need to memorize every piece of legislation. You don't even have to watch the news (although you might want to follow your local council's Instagram).

What you need is **curiosity, courage, and the willingness to start asking better questions.**

Who makes decisions in my town?

Where does the budget go?

What's getting voted on this year?

Who's in the room—and who's not?

When Icy Hearts Rule The World, Set it On Fire

Because once you start seeing how the system works, you *can't unsee it*. And once you realize how much power you *actually* have, especially in local politics, you won't want to sit it out ever again.

Running for office isn't about being political.

It's about being awake.

It's about giving a damn.

It's about showing up not because you have all the answers, but because you're willing to fight for better questions, and better outcomes.

You don't have to turn into a pundit. But you *do* have to turn on.

Because politics shapes your life, your family's life, your community's future. And whether you engage with it or not, it's already engaging with *you*.

So the next time you hear a woman say, "I'm not political," offer her something else:

"Maybe not yet. But what if you were?"

So many women hold back because we think leadership means expertise. That we need credentials or connections or a mentor in the Senate. But most of the people in office are learning on the fly. Half of them didn't know what a city charter was until six months into the job. Some of them still don't.

The difference is: they said yes.

They walked through the door.

They sat at the table, even when their hands were shaking.

And now? It's your turn.

You don't have to know everything. You just have to care enough to start.

You have a voice. A lived experience. A hundred moments that shaped how you see the world. That's not a weakness, that's *your* superpower. You know what it's like to juggle bills and grief and dreams and bureaucracy. You know how to lead with empathy, urgency, and truth. The system wasn't built for you, but it can't be rebuilt without you.

So here's what I'm asking:

Say yes to the spark.

Say yes to the version of you who keeps showing up, even when no one claps.

Say yes to exploring a life where power doesn't mean dominance, it means direction.

Say yes to stepping up, not because it's easy or glamorous, but because it's *yours.*

Set the world on fire. Let it light the way for others to join you.

2

LEADERSHIP LOOKS LIKE YOU

"Don't ever underestimate the importance you can have because history has shown us that courage can be contagious and hope can take on a life of its own."
— *Michelle Obama*

*L*et's be honest.

When most people hear the word *leader,* they don't picture someone like you.

They picture someone older. Louder. Taller. More "seasoned." Less... emotionally available. They picture a man in a dark suit with a firm handshake and a vague platform.

They do *not* picture you in your sweatpants, running a household, managing a team, advocating for your kid, running errands, and burning with ideas in the carpool line.

But here's the truth: Leadership already lives in you.

You've been leading this whole time—without the title, the paycheck, or the press release.

You've negotiated peace treaties over dinner tables.

You've managed budgets with nothing but note pad and miracles.

You've mobilized friends, family, and entire communities without calling it a campaign.

You've done what most leaders can't: You've led *without power*. Because in these situations, you believe in your own authority, and that's all it takes; knowing you have the authority to stand up for what you believe in, for what your community wants and needs. And that *authority*? There's nobody walking around granting it; it comes from you. You grant yourself the authority to step into any role you choose.

Now imagine what you could do with it.

One of the biggest lies women are told about leadership is that we're not ready.

Not experienced enough.

Not polished enough.

Not connected enough.

Not electable.

Let's pause right there: *Electable* is often just code for "makes powerful people comfortable."

If you're too loud, you're a problem.

If you're too quiet, you're weak.

If you have kids, you're distracted.

If you don't, you're cold.

If you show emotion, you're unstable.

If you don't, you're a robot.

You can't win that game—**so stop playing it.**

The truth is, no one is ever really "ready" for power.

And the people who *think* they are?

They're usually the last ones who should have it.

You, on the other hand, are in the arena of real life.

You've solved problems no policy paper ever anticipated.

You've led with your gut, your grit, and your love for your people.

That's leadership. Not just the kind we need, but the kind that's been missing.

There's this idea floating around that when women lead, they're "bringing something different to the table", like it's some sweet side dish to the main course of real leadership.

Let me say this as clearly as I can:

Women are not the seasoning. We are the substance.

Empathy isn't a soft skill. It's a leadership strategy.

Listening isn't a weakness. It's intelligence.

Collaboration isn't indecision. It's power that knows it doesn't have to dominate to move mountains.

When women lead, the room changes.

Budgets shift. Priorities realign. People get heard. Kids get fed. Policies get humane.

This isn't theory. It's data.

Studies show that when women are at the table—especially in local and state government, budgets become more equitable, crises are handled with greater care, and trust in public institutions actually *increases*.

So why aren't there more of us?

Because the system wasn't built for us, it was built to keep power in the hands of the few, favoring confidence over competence, and performance over presence.

But we're already rewriting that. Quietly, radically, from city halls to school boards to statehouses.

Let's talk about a word that tends to make people squirm: **Power.**

For a lot of folks, it sounds… sinister. Greedy. Corrupt. Like something only the ruthless chase, or the privileged inherit. We've seen power abused so often, it's easy to forget: **power itself is neutral.**

It's not inherently good or evil. It's a tool; like fire, like money, like a microphone. Its impact depends entirely on *who's holding it, and what they choose to do with it.*

The phrase "power corrupts" gets tossed around like a law of nature. But corruption isn't inevitable. It's a choice. And the truth is: **you can be powerful without being corruptible.**

You can hold power and still be kind. Still be honest. Still be deeply human. You can lead without bulldozing, build coalitions without selling out, and create systems that serve *all* of us, not just the few.

Power doesn't have to be something we fear or avoid. **It can be something we reclaim.** Something we channel into fairness, protection, accountability, and collective liberation.

So, don't shy away from power. **Shape it.** When good people hold power, **good things get done.**

The revolution has already begun.

It just doesn't look like a revolution.

It looks like *you*, filing your papers, knocking on doors, asking the right questions, refusing to sit down.

So let me ask you something.

Leadership Looks Like You

What if you've been a leader this whole time, and the only thing missing is the title?

What if leadership doesn't start when you get elected, but when you stop shrinking?

What if all the life you've lived, every job you've juggled, every boundary you've had to build, every injustice you've had to survive, was not a detour from power but preparation for it?

What if leadership looks like you, *right now*?

Not after a degree.

Not after your kids are older.

Not after you've "calmed down" or "figured it out" or "gotten it together."

But now.

Exactly as you are.

That's the beginning.

That's what changes the story, not just for you, but for every woman who's watching.

Because when you rise, they don't just cheer.

They remember they can rise, too.

And suddenly, leadership stops being something you chase.

It becomes something you *embody*.

Right here.

Right now.

As you are.

3

THE LOCAL ROOTS OF NATIONAL CHANGE:

THIS IS WHAT POWER LOOKS LIKE

> "The most common way people give up their power is by thinking they don't have any."
> — *Alice Walker*

*L*et's drop the modesty for a minute and speak plainly: **When women get into office, things get better.**

Not just warmer. Not just more "inclusive."

Better.

Budgets get smarter. Communities get safer. Families get fed.

Corruption drops. Collaboration goes up. Things move because we're not there for the power play. We're there to get shit done.

And not because we're magical creatures who float into meetings with fairy dust and maternal wisdom. But because we show up with something most political institutions have been missing: **lived reality.**

We don't lead to impress. We lead because we've lived the consequences of bad leadership.

That's why when women get in, especially women who've never been handed the mic before, they don't waste time.

They start cleaning house, passing policies, and asking better questions.

They start changing what leadership looks like, and what it *feels* like to be represented.

When women lead, they lead with purpose, and it shows.

Take the city councils and county boards that started addressing childcare not as a "women's issue" but as core economic infrastructure.

The state reps who looked at bloated criminal justice budgets and asked, "What if we funded prevention instead of punishment?"

The school board members who fought for free lunch, because no kid learns well while hungry.

These aren't just stories. They're ripple effects you can feel.

Let me tell you a secret: The real revolution doesn't start in Washington.

It starts in your town council chambers, your school board meetings, your sleepy state house committees. It starts on street corners and doorsteps and backyards where someone like you—sharp, tired, done waiting—finally decides to *run*.

And when she does? Everything shifts.

We've been sold a myth that change comes from the top. That national power is the real power. That the presidency or Congress is the prize.

The truth is, **federal politics is the parade. Local politics is the engine.**

The Local Roots of National Change:

Your city decides whether your neighbors get clean water.

Your school board shapes what the next generation learns about race, gender, and truth.

Your state legislature draws the maps that decide who even gets to vote, and who doesn't.

When women show up locally, they don't just shake the system. They rebuild it **from the ground up**.

We underestimate these roles because we've been *trained* to.

No one grows up saying, "I want to be on the zoning commission."

But the zoning commission decides whether a women's shelter gets built. Whether a highway splits a neighborhood in two. Whether your town will have green space or just another parking lot.

Policies shift because women tend to see the whole board.

We don't lead from silos, we lead from experience.

We know what it costs to make a household work, to survive on low pay, to navigate broken health systems, to be unseen in spaces that impact our lives.

And when that knowing enters the room in the form of a vote, a veto, a new ordinance, or a line in the budget, people notice.

Communities start to feel seen.

The gears of local government start turning with a little less ego and a lot more accountability.

And maybe for the first time, folks start showing up to town halls not just to *complain*, but to participate.

That's what happens when women hold power:

Government starts to *serve* again.

When a woman wins locally, she doesn't just get a seat, she opens a door.

That one win becomes ten, then a hundred. Once your community sees you do it, they start to believe they can too. Your campaign becomes a blueprint. Your courage becomes contagious. That's how waves begin.

And here's what no one will put in the brochure:

Most national leaders? They started right here.

On a city council. A school board. A housing committee.

They cut their teeth on potholes and policy binders and angry town hall meetings before ever touching the Capitol steps. These so-called "stepping stones" aren't lesser, they're launchpads.

Local races are the leadership pipeline. They build the bench. They grow governance from the inside out, the way *all real things grow*: with roots, not hype.

And it's not just political infrastructure.

It's *cultural*.

When women lead at the local level, communities start to look, feel, and function differently.

People start to see a mother of three leading a committee meeting and think: *That's leadership, too.*

They hear a formerly incarcerated woman advocating for reentry services and realize: *This is what representation sounds like.*

They watch a queer Black woman pass a housing ordinance and begin to understand: *Maybe this system could finally start working for all of us.*

That kind of visibility is electric.

It re-teaches the public what leadership is—and who it belongs to.

The Local Roots of National Change:

And girl, it belongs to you.

When women win at the local level—when they step into power with all their imperfection, their clarity, their lived truth—they alter the course of lives in ways most people will never see on the news. But the ripple is real.

It looks like a domestic violence survivor is finally getting housing because a councilwoman refused to let her fall through the cracks.

It looks like a trans teen feeling seen for the first time in school because their district finally passed an inclusive policy.

It looks like a mom not having to choose between rent and medicine because a woman in power fought for a local subsidy that no one else would touch.

That's the work.

Not glamorous. Not always loud. But lasting. And when you do it, not if, but *when*, you won't just be writing policy. You'll be writing a legacy. Because the truth is, someone is always watching you lead. Your kids. Your neighbors. A woman you don't even know yet who's waiting for proof that people like her belong in power. And when they see you hold your seat with integrity, when they see you vote with a spine, when they see you show up over and over again in a system designed to wear you down, something shifts in them, too.

This is how we move the world.

Not all at once. Not from the top down.

But woman by woman, city by city, seat by seat.

Let's stop pretending we don't know what happens when women take the lead. We know.

We've seen it in the small, quiet ways, like when a woman in city government adjusts the bus routes so working moms don't have to wait in the cold with their kids. And we've seen it in world-shifting, country-defining ways, like when a woman prime minister locks down her nation with care, compassion, and clarity and saves thousands of lives.

Women in leadership aren't "nice-to-have."

They're a necessity.

And not just because it feels good to say we elected a woman, or because we "need more voices at the table." (Though we do, obviously). But because when women lead, especially in public life, **things change. And they change fast.**

Take New Zealand.

During the Covid pandemic, Prime Minister Jacinda Ardern didn't posture. She didn't stall. She acted. Early lockdowns. Clear communication. Daily briefings that felt more like a conversation than a press stunt. Her approval ratings soared, not because she catered to everyone, but because she told the truth, quickly and with empathy. New Zealand came through the crisis with one of the lowest death rates in the developed world. That's not just leadership. That's woman-led governance in action: swift, compassionate, decisive.

Look at Finland.

With a government led by Sanna Marin and a coalition of young, progressive female ministers, Finland didn't just talk about equity, they implemented it. Their policies focused on family leave, education, climate change, and fair wages. Their leadership isn't flashy. It's functional. It's built to work for people, *all* people, not just the elite or the loudest voices in the room.

And Rwanda.

Yes, Rwanda. After genocide decimated the country, women stepped into politics in unprecedented numbers. Today, Rwanda has one of the highest percentages of women in parliament in the world, over 60%. The result? Gains in education, healthcare, and infrastructure. A dramatic reduction in maternal and infant mortality. Massive improvements in gender equity. Rwanda became a case study in national healing through inclusive leadership.

When Women Lead, the Focus Shifts

We stop fixating on abstract power and start building systems that **actually serve people.**

We spend less time grandstanding and more time governing.

We stop rewarding ego and start rewarding outcomes.

When women lead, we don't just ask, *"What's the bottom line?"*

We ask, *"What's the human cost?"*

We ask, *"Who hasn't been heard?"*

We ask, *"What kind of future do we want to create?"*

Women are more likely to prioritize healthcare, education, childcare, voting access, and public safety. They build coalitions, not cults of personality. They listen longer. They interrupt less. And they tend to govern for the long term, not just the next news cycle. That's not speculation. The evidence is everywhere.

And It's Not Just Abroad—It's Here.

Across the U.S., from mayors to governors to state legislators, women are changing the game. They're pushing forward policies that protect families, support teachers, fund public transit, and ensure reproductive rights. They are de-normalizing the toxic idea that politics must be ruthless to be effective. They're doing it differently—and *better.*

You don't have to move to Washington to move the country forward.

You can do it from your neighborhood. From your school district. From your county clerk's office or your city hall.

You can do it without leaving your kids, your career, your messy, beautiful, real life.

You can build a political legacy and still make it to soccer practice—or don't, maybe you're a swim mom, or a no-kid, book-club, dog-park, backyard-garden type. Doesn't matter. There's no one way to lead.

The point is: this can fit into *your* life.

Because you're not here to serve the system.

You're here to *rebuild it*.

And when you run—especially when you run locally—you're not just fixing potholes or passing resolutions.

You're writing a new story.

For your city.

For your state.

For the women who come after you, who need to see it done before they believe it's possible.

So if you've been waiting for a sign that your leadership matters, this is it.

If you've been wondering whether starting "small" is worth your time, this is your answer: **There is nothing small about changing everything.**

Run for office.

Run where you are.

Run now.

Because when women envision a society, they don't just see numbers and laws. They see people. They see their neighbors. They see the kids in their own schools. They feel the impact in their bones. And they know that governance isn't about winning —it's about **creating a life that's more livable for more people.**

Because from the ground up is how we build a new America, and you are already the foundation.

So Let's Be Clear: If you've ever doubted whether one person, *one woman*, can change a system, the answer is yes.

Yes, she can.

Yes, you can.

When women lead, society doesn't just shift.

It *transforms*.

Faster. Fairer. More just. More kind. More of what this world so desperately needs.

So don't let anyone tell you the game can't be changed. **We are the ones changing it. Right now.**

The revolution doesn't need permission. It needs addresses, agendas, and women who know the power of showing up.

4

WHAT THE HELL AM I EVEN RUNNING FOR?

> "Any woman who understands the problems of running a home will be nearer to understanding the problems of running a country."
> — *Margaret Thatcher*

By now, you might be thinking:

"Okay, okay, I'm fired up, I care, I'm in. But… what exactly am I supposed to *run for*?"

That's a fair question.

Because the political system is a bit like an old attic: dusty, overcomplicated, and full of weird titles no one explains.

Recorder of deeds? Water district board? Township trustee?

What even *are* these things?

And more importantly, who the hell is running them right now?

(Hint: it's often a guy who's been there for twenty years and hasn't updated his website, or his values, since dial-up.)

Here's the truth they don't advertise on civics posters:

There are hundreds of seats of power in your city, county, and state that impact your life every day, and most people have *no idea* who holds them.

That's where you come in.

Let's talk about the seats no one brags about at cocktail parties, but that actually shape people's lives.

School board. City council. County commission. Planning and zoning. Public utility districts. State legislature.

These might not sound sexy, but they are where policy lives and breathes. These seats decide what's funded, what's ignored, what gets built, what gets banned, and who gets to participate in shaping their own community.

These are the positions that determine:

Whether your neighbor's water bill triples.

Whether teachers get a raise or another set of empty "thank-you" notes.

Whether your city creates affordable housing or keeps building luxury condos no one lives in.

And you don't need to climb a ladder to get there.

You can start right here, right now, with what you know, and what you care about.

If you're fired up about education? Look at the school board.

If you care about environmental justice? Start with your local water or conservation district.

If your neighborhood's been neglected for decades? That's city council territory.

What the Hell Am I Even Running For?

If you want to shape the state budget, protect healthcare access, and make voting easier? State legislature, baby.

You don't have to run for Congress to make history. You can run for mosquito abatement and still raise some hell (and some funding).

It's not about the prestige. It's about the power, and using it where it matters most.

Let's bust another myth while we're here: Local doesn't mean small.

Running for your local school board might not get you a national news segment, but it *will* give you a vote on what kids in your community learn, what teachers get paid, and how inclusive your district actually is.

Running for city council won't get you invited to fancy dinners in D.C., but you'll have a say in how your town grows, how your neighbors live, and whether your community is thriving, or barely surviving.

You don't need to run for something that looks impressive. You need to run for something that feels like yours.

This isn't about checking a box.

It's about planting a flag. It's about seeing a gap in leadership, a place where people aren't being served, heard, or protected, and deciding, *I can do that. I will do that.*

So, don't get caught up in whether it sounds like enough.

Ask yourself:

Where do I feel pulled?

What problems do I keep ranting about over dinner?

Where do my skills and fire meet the community's needs?

That's your lane.

That's your race.

And the moment you name it, even if it feels wild or scary or way too grown-up, you begin to shift.

You stop waiting for someone else to fix it.

You start becoming the one who does.

There's no "right" seat.

There's only the one that calls to you.

The one that keeps tugging at your gut every time you see a bad policy get passed, or a good person give up, or a whole neighborhood get ignored again.

You don't need to run for what sounds important.

You need to run for what is important to you, to your people, to the place you live and love.

Because the most powerful campaigns aren't built on ambition.

They're built on alignment.

When you run from that place, from clarity, from conviction, you don't need to fake it.

You don't need to script your values or water yourself down to make your candidacy "palatable."

You just tell the truth.

You say, *Here's what I care about. Here's what I've seen. Here's what I'm going to do.*

And people feel it.

That's when doors start opening.

That's when support starts building.

That's when the whole thing stops being hypothetical and starts being *real*.

So go ahead. Ask the question. Not, *Am I ready?* But, *What seat fits the size of my soul?*

And when you feel the answer, even if it's just a flicker, follow it.

Now let's talk brass tacks, because not every elected seat demands the same hours, the same energy, or offers the same paycheck.

Some roles are part-time, like school board or city council in smaller municipalities. These might require a few meetings a month and some community events, leaving plenty of room for your day job, your family, and your sanity. Others, like state representative or county commissioner, can become full-time commitments, especially during legislative sessions or budget season. And then there are positions that are full-time, both in pay and in expectation: mayor, judge, state senator, etc....

And let's be honest: compensation is all over the place. Some roles offer stipends so small you'd lose money on gas just driving to the meetings. Others come with a livable salary, healthcare benefits, and a real staff. And still others fall somewhere in between—enough to matter, but not enough to live on.

But here's another truth no one puts on the brochure: your impact isn't measured in hours worked or dollars earned. It's measured in how well you listen, how clearly you see the needs of your people, and how courageously you fight to create solutions that work for everyone. That's the work that matters. That's what gets remembered.

So yes, do your research. Ask what the role requires. Know the calendar, the compensation, the expectations. But then—check in with yourself. Ask, Is this worth my energy? Can I serve well and still stay well?

Because martyrdom is not a leadership strategy. Running yourself into the ground doesn't make you important, it makes you unavailable. You can't serve your people well if you're drowning. You can't show up with vision if you're running on fumes.

So your job, before and during public service, is this: create a life with enough balance that your leadership comes from overflow, not depletion. Your community deserves your best, but so do you. You're allowed to protect your time, your peace, your joy. In fact, it's required.

5

HOW TO ACTUALLY GET ON THE BALLOT

"The most effective way to do it, is to do it."
— Amelia Earhart

Okay, let's demystify this thing.

So you've decided to run—or you're at least saying it out loud in the mirror with one eyebrow raised. You feel the fire. You know what seat you want. But then reality comes knocking with a long list of questions like:

How do I actually get on the ballot?

What forms do I fill out?

Do I need a treasurer?

Do I need to raise a million dollars by Thursday?

Is there a secret political handshake I don't know?

Let me say this gently but firmly: You are smart enough to figure this out even if it feels overwhelming right now, especially if you've never done anything like this before.

Because the system wants you to feel overwhelmed. That confusion? That bureaucracy? That sea of PDFs and poorly designed government websites? That's not a coincidence. That's a barrier.

But here's the good news: it's a barrier you can walk through.

And I'm going to show you how. Here we go!

Step One: Find the Rules—Then Actually Read Them

Every state and locality has its own process for getting on the ballot. That means there's no one-size-fits-all magic checklist—but there *is* always a clear set of rules.

Start with your **local election authority**—your county clerk, board of elections, or the secretary of state's website. They are legally required to publish:

- Filing deadlines
- Eligibility requirements
- The exact number of petition signatures (if applicable)
- Fee amounts (sometimes it's free, sometimes not)
- What forms you need and when

Pro tip: Call them. Yes, pick up the phone. Election officials are usually civil servants, not partisan gatekeepers. Most of them will walk you through the process if you ask clearly and kindly.

And if they treat you like you don't belong?

Congratulations. You've just had your first taste of why you *do* belong.

Step Two: File Like a Grown-Ass Woman

Filing usually involves two parts:

1. **Declaring your candidacy**
2. **Filing to appear on the ballot**

Sometimes they're combined. Sometimes they're separate. You'll fill out basic info, sign under penalty of perjury, and (if needed) drop a filing fee or petition sheet on someone's desk like a boss.

This moment is bigger than it seems.

You're not just signing paperwork, you're making a *declaration*.

You're saying, "I'm running," in ink.

And no matter what happens next, no one can take that from you.

Step Three: Open a Campaign Bank Account

As soon as you start spending or raising money, you need a separate bank account, because your campaign is a legal entity. It has its own rules, its own reporting requirements, and yes, its own paperwork party.

Most candidates start by:

- Applying for an **EIN** (Employer Identification Number) from the IRS (free, fast, online)
- Taking that EIN to a bank and opening a **campaign checking account**
- Assigning a **treasurer** (this can be you at first, but it's good to find a trusted numbers person)

Don't overthink it. Do it right. Keep your receipts. And don't use Venmo for campaign donations unless you're 100% sure you've read the fine print in your state's ethics laws.

Step Four: Raise Money Without Losing Yourself

Yes, you're gonna need money.

Even small local races require some cash for signs, mailers, a website, and that one local newspaper ad your aunt insists everyone reads (she's probably right).

But here's what you need to remember:

Fundraising isn't begging. It's inviting people to invest in change.

You're not asking for charity. You're asking for partnership. You're saying, *I'm doing something bold. Want to be part of it?*

Start close:

- Friends, family, neighbors
- Former coworkers, PTA parents, community members
- People who've seen you lead already, even informally

And yes, you'll have to ask. On the phone. In DMs. Over coffee.

Will it be awkward at first? Probably.

Will it get easier? Absolutely.

Set a clear goal. Use your voice. Be honest about what the money will fund. And always, *always*, send a thank-you note.

This isn't about chasing rich donors. It's about building a circle of support that believes in *you*.

Step Five: Build a Team That Feels Like a Forcefield

You do not have to do this alone. Nor should you.

Start with people who know and love you, folks who aren't afraid to tell you when your flyer looks weird or your slogan needs work. Look for:

- A **treasurer** (someone responsible, detail-oriented, not afraid of spreadsheets
- A **volunteer coordinator** (someone who knows how to rally people without scaring them)
- A **campaign manager** (if possible—a strategic thinker who can keep things moving)
- At the beginning, roles will blur. People will wear many hats. That's okay. What matters is trust.

- You don't need professionals right away. You need *believers.*
- People who see what you're building and say, "Let me help."

You can train skills. You can't fake loyalty.

Step Six: Run Your Race Like It's *Yours*

Once you've filed, opened your account, raised a few dollars, and wrangled your first crew, you're in it.

This is where some people start building a brand, others build a plan, and some just panic and make a TikTok. All valid.

But here's what I want you to remember: **You get to run this race in a way that honors your life.** You don't have to go broke or burn out to prove you care. You don't have to pretend you've got a twenty-person staff if it's just you, your cousin, and your laptop in a coffee shop. You don't have to act like you know everything (no one does).

You're allowed to build this campaign with clarity, boundaries, and soul.

Start with your calendar. Mark your filing deadline, early voting dates, election day, and any big community events. Then build a timeline backwards. Set weekly goals. Give yourself breaks. Bake in *real life*, your work schedule, your kids, your partner, your dog who gets anxiety when the doorbell rings.

This isn't about being superhuman. It's about being steady.

You can show up with heart, humor, and tenacity *and* still get eight hours of sleep, you can run a serious campaign without becoming a robot. You can be powerful *without* losing your center. In fact, that might just be your greatest asset.

6

YOU CAN'T SHAME A WOMAN WHO'S ALREADY DONE THE WORK

> "It's not your job to like me, it's mine."
> — *Byron Katie*

*L*et's not pretend.

Running for office means putting yourself out there in a way that can feel equal parts terrifying and infuriating. You are no longer just a person. You're a *public* person.

And once you declare your candidacy, hell, sometimes even just hint at it, *they come.*

The critics.

The internet trolls.

The "well-meaning" friends who suddenly have strong opinions about your tone, your timeline, and your haircut.

The distant relatives who pop up on Facebook with conspiracy theories and Bible verses about a "woman's place."

For many women, especially women of color, queer women, poor women, anyone who's ever sat outside the margins of traditional power, the backlash isn't theoretical. It's real. And it's exhausting.

Remember this: They don't come for you because you're weak. They come because they *see your strength*. And it makes them nervous.

No question: the fear is valid.

Putting yourself in the public eye, especially as a woman in a political space, can feel like standing naked in a snowstorm while strangers throw tomatoes and unsolicited advice.

You'll worry about your safety, your family, and your reputation.

You'll second-guess your voice, your past, your words, your wardrobe.

You'll ask yourself: *Am I strong enough to take the hits?*

And the answer isn't some glowing meme about bravery.

The answer is: you don't have to be invincible. You just have to be anchored.

Anchored to your values.

Anchored to your people.

Anchored to your *why*.

Because they will try to knock you off-center.

They will question your motives, your morals, your experience, and your tone.

They'll tell you to be less angry.

They'll tell you to smile more.

They'll say, "You're just doing this for attention," as if women haven't been fighting to be *heard* for generations.

So protect your energy like your future depends on it—because it does.

If you feel like maybe you have too many skeletons in your closet, I've got news: in the old world of politics, perfection was currency. You wanted to run? You needed to polish up that résumé until it sparkled, erase the mess, bury the chaos, and pray no one looked too hard at what you'd been through.

But that game? It's done.

This is a new era. And in this era, what used to disqualify you is the very reason you *belong* in the room. The broken parts, the off-ramps, the late-night cries on bathroom floors. The stretch marks, the credit card debt, the addiction you faced down and survived. The relationships you stayed in too long, the ones you had to run from, the messy years where you weren't sure who the hell you were. That's your gold.

This world doesn't need more polished politicians. It needs truth-tellers. People who've walked through fire and came out the other side *not untouched—but forged.*

You don't need a clean sheet. You need a beating heart, a lived life, and the guts to speak plainly. Because here's the truth: people are tired. Tired of being preached to by folks who've never been knocked flat. Tired of being judged by those who've never had to make an impossible decision just to keep their kids fed. Tired of systems built by people who've never had to navigate one just to survive.

You know who builds better systems? People who've been broken by them.

And let's not pretend this is easy. It takes courage to step forward with your full story. The shame can still whisper: *Who do you think you are?* But you get to answer back: *I'm someone who's lived. I'm someone who's learned. And I am done pretending I have to be flawless to lead.*

Flawed leaders see things others miss. We see nuance. We see struggle. We see people, not just policy. **And when we lead, we lead with humanity.**

You don't owe the world a version of yourself that's been bleached of pain. You owe it your *whole* self, honest, complicated, and resilient. That's what people are starving for.

Realness.

Grit.

Someone who gets it.

Your scars are not stains. They are maps. They show you where you've been, and they help others find their way out.

So if you've ever thought, *"I could never run, not with my past,"*—let me tell you something: You were *made* for this. Not despite your story. But *because* of it.

You are the second chance.

You are the return from the dark.

You are proof that people change, that healing is possible, that power doesn't have to come from privilege.

Don't dim your light to fit into some outdated mold. **Shatter it.** Walk in with your full self and say: *Here I am. Here's what I've seen. Here's what I know. I'm ready to serve.*

Take breaks from the noise.

Create sacred spaces where no one is allowed to talk politics, or critique you, or treat your ambition like a problem. Surround yourself with people who remind you who the hell you are.

Because on the days when the internet is loud and the voice in your head is louder, you'll need someone who can say, *"No, you're not crazy. This matters. Keep going."*

You Can't Shame a Woman Who's Already Done the Work

Here's what you need to know: **Truth is disarming.**

We've been conditioned to believe that leadership means having all the answers. But the most compelling leaders, the ones who actually *move* people, aren't perfect. They're honest.

So when they come for you, come back with the truth. "I don't know" isn't weakness, it's honesty. What matters is what comes next: *"I'll find out and circle back."* Not defensiveness. Not spin. Just truth.

Say: *Yes, I'm angry. And here's why.*

Say: *No, I don't have a long political resume. But I've been living in this district my whole damn life, and I know what's broken.*

Say: *I'm not running because I'm flawless. I'm running because I'm done waiting.*

You don't need to brand yourself into blandness.

You don't need to shrink yourself into civility.

Lead with your story, raw edges and all.

Lead with your questions, your fire, your fierce love for your people.

Your authenticity is not a liability. It's your power source.

And guess what? You're not for everyone. That's fine.

Let them be uncomfortable.

Let them call you names.

Let them misquote you, underestimate you, mock your tone.

You are not here to be digestible.

You are here to *lead*.

And that means choosing your own voice over their approval, over and over again.

Courage doesn't always look like fire.

Sometimes it looks like showing up to a meeting when you'd rather hide.

Sometimes it looks like speaking calmly while your heart is pounding.

Sometimes it's just... staying. Not quitting. Saying the hard thing anyway.

And here's the real secret they won't tell you in any campaign training: You don't have to feel brave to be brave. You just have to keep moving in the direction of what matters more than your fear. Because on the other side of fear is momentum. And on the other side of momentum is power. And on the other side of power, your power, are the people who are watching you, needing you, quietly rooting for you to make it through the mess so they can believe they can too.

So let them come.

Let them question, dismiss, distort, project.

You're not here to play small.

You're not here to avoid criticism.

You're here to change what's possible.

And every time you stand up anyway, voice shaking, knees knocking, but still standing, you make space for someone else to do the same.

That's not politics. That's impact. It's what you leave behind that continues to influence others, the fire you pass forward.

7

THE POLITICS OF BECOMING HER

"A woman with a voice is by definition a strong woman. But the search to find that voice can be remarkably difficult."
— *Melinda Gates*

No one tells you that running for office is going to ruin you.

Ruin the version of you that was waiting politely to be invited to the table. Ruin the girl who was trying so hard to be liked she forgot to be powerful. Ruin the woman who thought she had to choose between being respected and being real.

Running doesn't just change your schedule. It changes your shape.

It stretches your voice, literally and metaphorically. You'll hear yourself say things you never thought you'd say out loud: "I'm running for office." "That's not true, and I won't stand for it." "Please stop tweeting that I'm a lizard in a pantsuit."

And then you'll start saying things you *do* believe. You'll speak them with your whole chest, from somewhere ancient and alive inside you. Not because you're trying to prove yourself, but because you've finally decided to belong to yourself.

This is the part no one talks about enough: You don't run for office just to serve your community. You run to **become the kind of woman your community never knew they were allowed to believe in**.

And here's the wildest part. Once you say it, once you claim your place in the public sphere, you can't un-know what it feels like to be powerful.

Even if you don't win this time, even if you step away from politics later, something in you has changed its posture permanently. You stand differently. You ask different questions. You stop apologizing when you walk into a room.

Because you've tasted it, what it means to step forward with no one's permission but your own. You're acting on your own authority and this change isn't subtle. It shows up in ways that might unsettle the people around you.

People who loved you soft and agreeable may start to fidget now that you're bold and clear.

People who were used to leading you might not know how to follow you.

And those who were always secretly threatened by your light? Oh, honey. Buckle up.

You will become inconvenient to small-minded people.

You will also become magnetic to the ones who've been waiting for someone just like you.

This is the unspoken politics of becoming her: **It costs something. But it gives you everything.**

It gives you a voice you trust more than anyone's approval.

It gives you a spine you didn't know you had.

It gives you a vision of yourself that makes the past you look like a draft copy.

But becoming her, the future you who owns her voice, her power, her full damn presence, comes with some grief.

No one talks about the grief.

You might find yourself mourning a version of you who stayed small to stay safe. You might miss the ease of being underestimated. There's something almost cozy about invisibility until you realize it's been costing you your life.

You'll also grieve relationships that can't come with you.

The friend who changes the subject every time you talk about your campaign.

The partner who says they support you but starts picking fights before big events.

The family member who thinks this all just means you've gotten "too political."

They don't always leave with a dramatic exit. Some of them just fade. The text frequency drops. The energy shifts. You stop contorting yourself to make other people comfortable, and suddenly, surprise, they were only there for the contortionist act.

That hurts.

It's supposed to.

Because what's growing in you is no longer available for rent.

You're not asking if you're allowed to be big anymore. You're building a life that *requires* it.

And that kind of bigness will always trigger the people still trying to shrink themselves.

So you grieve. You breathe. You keep going.

And in the empty spaces where old dynamics used to sit, new ones form. You find your people, the ones who don't flinch when you speak the truth. The ones who hear your ideas and say, "Go bigger." The ones who show up, not just for your events, but for your becoming.

What no one prepares you for is how good it feels. Not in some polished, patriotic, press-conference way. In a blood-deep, soul-loud, *finally* kind of way.

You stop filtering. You stop folding yourself into someone else's version of appropriate, and suddenly, your creativity returns. Your laughter gets louder. Your ideas stop asking for permission and start kicking down doors. You remember that your voice is not just powerful, it's *original.*

You start to see leadership not as a costume you put on, but as a form of art.

Politics becomes an extension of your creative self, your spiritual self, your unapologetic self. It stops being about whether you're qualified. It starts being about whether you're *called.*

Here's the thing: There are women out there sitting on school boards, city councils, state senates—who never thought they belonged in politics until they showed up and did it anyway.

There are policies being written by women who used to shrink themselves at dinner parties.

There are laws being passed by women who once convinced

themselves they were "just moms," "just teachers," "just working-class girls from small towns."

And there is you.

Not because you were trained for this.

But because you *were born* for this.

So run. Not just for office, but for *yourself.*

Run toward the version of you who doesn't negotiate her worth, who doesn't dilute her fire, who stands up not just to be counted, but to *count*.

She's not waiting anymore.

She's here.

8

VICTORY IS JUST THE BEGINNING

"We can do no great things, only small things with great love."
— *Mother Theresa*

So... you won.

You hugged your team. You cried into your champagne. You peeled your eyelashes off and ate french fries in the parking lot while staring at the night sky, wondering what the hell you just did.

And now?

Now you get to do the job.

Here's what no one tells you during the campaign: winning is not the final boss level. It's the first day of a new life, one that will ask even more of you than the race did.

Governing isn't just about policy.

It's about presence.

It's about sitting in rooms you once imagined from the outside, and realizing *you are the system now.*

And what you do with that realization will define the mark you leave on the world.

Governing is slower than campaigning. Less glamorous. More bureaucratic. There are no yard signs. No rallies. No music swelling as you walk into a room. Instead, there are committee meetings that drag on for hours, 400-page budget binders, and constituents who call you on your personal cell to ask why their trash wasn't picked up.

But this? This is the real work. Because now, you're not just dreaming about change, you *are* the one with the vote, the voice, the responsibility.

You're the one who can move a policy forward, or kill it with a well-placed question.

You're the one who can push for accountability, or quietly let it slide.

This is where your values stop being talking points and start becoming choices that create a ripple effect.

Do you fight for that line item in the budget when you know it might cost you political capital?

Do you challenge that colleague's proposal, even though it's "not the hill to die on"?

Do you make the calls, write the amendments, do the *unglamorous* work that real change demands?

Because governing isn't about your ego. It's about your **staying power.**

Can you keep showing up when no one's clapping?

Can you push back when your voice is the only dissent in the room?

You didn't run just to win. You ran because you knew things needed to change. Now's your chance to do it.

There's a moment, after the campaign dust settles, after the handshakes and the oaths and the awkward photo ops, where it hits you: *Now I have to lead.*

Not just speak. Not just fight. **Lead.**

And real leadership, especially in civic life, isn't about commanding attention. It's about *earning trust*. It's about **holding complexity**, honoring diverse voices, and keeping your values clear while building consensus across competing needs.

You don't have to become someone else to do this well. You *do* have to become more of who you are at your best, honest, steady, listening even when it's hard, showing up even when it's uncomfortable.

Because unlike business leadership, where the bottom line is profit and the playbook is speed, or nonprofit leadership, where your mission is clearly defined and your supporters are largely aligned, **civic leadership lives in the wild terrain of contradiction, conflict, and compromise.**

It's not about optimizing. It's about *representing*. Not just your base. Not just your donors. Not just the people who agree with you on Tuesday and yell at you on Thursday. All of them. Even the ones who didn't vote for you. Even the ones who never will.

Civic leadership means waking up each day and saying: *What's best for the most people—not just what's easiest or most popular?*

It means listening to constituents who fundamentally disagree with you, and still treating them with dignity. Not because they're right, but because the moment you stop listening, you become what you swore to change.

It means staying rooted in your values while knowing when to bend, not break, for the greater good. There will be times when you have to choose between the ideal and the possible. And you'll need to know the difference between selling out, and *moving the needle*.

It means saying no to what's flashy in favor of what's fair. You'll be tempted by headlines, by photo ops, by big initiatives that sound great in speeches but do little for real people. Resist the urge to perform. Lean into the power to *serve*.

It means becoming fluent in translation.

Policy into plain language.

Community outrage into legislative clarity.

Constituent stories into budget priorities.

You are the bridge between systems and people. The language you use matters more than you think.

And most of all, it means representing more than just your own voice. Your job isn't to be the loudest. It's to listen, synthesize, decide, and stay accountable.

Let's look at a few **real-world leadership examples** of civic leadership in action—these women have navigated complexity, conflict, or quiet revolution with humility, clarity, and vision. They demonstrate *how* civic leadership actually works in practice—especially when it isn't perfect, but still powerful.

Lori Chavez-DeRemer (U.S. Secretary of Labor)

A moderate Republican Latina, formerly a U.S. House Representative a traditionally blue district, Chavez-DeRemer represents a deeply divided constituency. Instead of choosing sides, she built her office around *communication and practical wins*. From improving transportation access to addressing the opioid crisis, she focuses on issues that matter to both parties, listens carefully, and isn't afraid to take heat from her own side when necessary.

Her leadership in action? Listening across the aisle, standing in discomfort, and working for the common good instead of the party line.

Stacy Abrams (Georgia)

After her terms as the Minority Leader of the Georgia House of Representatives and a Member of the Georgia House of Representatives, Abrams lost the gubernatorial race in 2018, but she didn't disappear; she doubled down. She built Fair Fight Action to address voter suppression, modernized voter registration, and helped shift an entire state's political landscape.

Her leadership in action? Losing with integrity, building infrastructure from the ground up, and expanding access to democracy for future leaders.

Anne Hidalgo (Mayor of Paris, France)

Hidalgo has turned Paris into a global example of urban transformation, prioritizing bike infrastructure, environmental sustainability, and family-friendly public spaces. Despite backlash from car-centric groups and developers, she's remained clear-eyed in her vision for a greener, more livable city.

Her leadership in action? Vision-driven planning, resilience in the face of criticism, and making cities safer and more equitable for everyone—not just the wealthy.

London Breed (Mayor of San Francisco)

Raised in public housing, Breed lead one of America's most complex cities with a deep understanding of poverty, equity, and bureaucracy. Her leadership has included tough pandemic decisions, housing battles, and public safety debates. While not without controversy, she consistently emphasizes *lived experience*, representation, and community connection as the heart of her leadership.

Her leadership in action? Balancing policy and identity, leading from life experience, and showing up even when it's messy.

Sanna Marin (Former Prime Minister of Finland)

Marin made headlines as the world's youngest sitting prime minister, but it was her crisis-leadership during Covid and her unapologetically progressive stance on gender equality that defined her. She governed with a coalition of women, expanded parental leave, and held the line on democratic values, even as far-right critics tried to reduce her leadership to her age and femininity.

Her leadership in action? Feminine power without apology, consensus-driven governance, and using youth and empathy as strengths—not weaknesses.

Each of these women led differently. But the throughline? They listened. They stood tall in tough rooms. They remembered who they were there for. **They led from values, not vanity.**

That's the kind of leadership this country needs more of. That's what you're being called toward.

You're not there to project perfection. You're there to build something better than what came before. That takes humility. It takes courage. And it takes a commitment not to be right all the time, but to get it right over time.

You were elected to serve. That doesn't mean being a blank slate, or a mouthpiece, or a "both-sides" apologist. It means becoming a channel, not for your personal agenda or the loudest voice in the room, but for **insight, clarity, and meaningful action.**

It means taking the **frustration** you hear from your constituents and turning it into *focused pressure*, the kind that moves policy, shifts priorities, and signals, "We're watching." It means taking the **hope** you hear, the quiet dreams for better schools, safer neighborhoods, fairer rules, and turning it into *momentum*. Not just platitudes or promises, but traction. And it means taking the **stories** you hear in parking lots, town halls, and kitchen-table conversations, and shaping policy that sees people not as numbers, but as neighbors.

That's civic leadership.

It's making sure **no one gets steamrolled just because they weren't in the room**, because you were in the room, and you saw them coming. It's using your seat to **amplify the unheard**, not just the most powerful, the most organized, or the most well-funded. It's knowing when to **pause before you speak**, when to ask a better question instead of rushing into certainty, when to *build something lasting* instead of bulldozing through just to prove a point.

It's not about being perfect.

It's about being **present**.

Being **available to grow**.

Being the kind of leader people can trust to **think deeply, act wisely, and admit when she doesn't know, but go find the answer anyway**.

And yes, get your talking points sharp. Master your budget. Learn the statutes, the charters, the process. Understand how government *actually* works, and where it fails people.

But **never forget**: This is a relationship. Not a show.

You are here to build trust with the people you serve. Not because they need a savior. But because they deserve a representative who **sees them**, listens without condescension, fights without theatrics, and stays rooted even when the political winds shift.

That's the bar.

Not perfection.

But **presence, principle, and persistence**.

And if you can hold that? You won't just lead. You'll **change what leadership looks like** for everyone who comes next.

The campaign trail tests your energy.

But governing? That tests your *center*.

You'll be pulled in a thousand directions, by colleagues, constituents, staff, the media, your own damn calendar. Everyone will want something. Everyone will think it's urgent.

But here's the thing, just because you're in power doesn't mean you have to become part of the machine. In fact, the best leaders resist it.

They remember who they were before the title.

They create space between their soul and the system.

They slow down long enough to ask: *Is this aligned? Or just expected?*

Because if you're not careful, politics will try to shape you into something smoother, safer, more acceptable. It'll tempt you to make peace instead of progress. It'll praise your "professionalism" when you stay quiet, and question your "temperament" when you raise hell.

But you didn't get here to be polite. You didn't win just to fit in. You are here to stay rooted, stay clear, and stay human.

Protect your time. Keep your rituals. Have your people. Step away when you need to. Speak with your full voice, even when it trembles. And don't forget to breathe, to laugh, to live a life outside your office, your inbox, your next vote.

Because the woman who ran?

She's still in there.

And she's the one who's going to keep this whole thing honest.

It's easy to think the real win was election night. **The real win is every moment you lead with integrity in a space that wasn't built for you.**

Every time you advocate for your people, not your reputation.

Every time you cast a vote that aligns with your values, even when it's not politically safe.

Every time you slow a bad decision, open a new conversation, or simply show up as *yourself* in a room where women weren't expected to lead, let alone lead like *this*.

That's transformational leadership. That's what changes how power looks, feels, and functions for the next generation.

You are not just governing a district or a ward or a zip code. You are shaping the blueprint for what's possible in every city hall, statehouse, and committee room that follows.

And when your term ends, whether it's one year or twenty, you'll walk away not with a perfectly polished record, but with something deeper: A life of service on your own terms. A story you're proud of. A legacy you didn't just inherit, but *built*.

Because power isn't about the title. It's about what you do once you have it.

And you? You care enough to get it right.

you cry in the car, rip the signs down, feel like you let people down, or worse, feel like you confirmed every secret fear that said you weren't meant for this in the first place?

Let's go ahead and say it: Losing sucks, it hurts.

It's not just disappointing. It's personal. Unlike other jobs you apply for, running for office isn't just about your résumé, it's about *you*. Your beliefs. Your story. Your face on a yard sign.

So when people say no, when a district or a town or even just a few hundred votes say, "Not this time,"—it can feel like rejection on a soul-deep level.

> "Nothing has transformed my life more than realizing that it's a waste of time to evaluate my worthiness by weighing the reaction of the people in the stands."
>
> — Brené Brown, Daring Greatly: How the Courage to Be Vulnerable Transforms the Way We Live, Love, Parent, and Lead

I'll be honest with you: **losing an election doesn't mean you failed.**

It means you had the courage to show up. To stand for something. To put your name on the line and say, *"I believe this can be better."*

And ruminating over what people think, or what they might've thought, is like **standing in an empty theater, replaying a performance no one else is watching.** It won't change the ending. It just keeps you from moving on to the next act.

Every candidate, *every single one*, walks away with lessons, relationships, and power they didn't have before. You don't come out empty. You come out seasoned. **Sharpened. Clearer than ever.**

So take what you learned. Take what you felt. And *build something with it.*

Because the people who run again, stronger, wiser, more grounded, are often the ones who win the second time. Or the third. And even if you never file again, you'll have already done what most people never dare to do: You **showed up** when it counted.

You raised your hand and stepped into the light. And that's more than most people will ever do.

You know what losing also means? It means you learned how to run a campaign. It means you connected with hundreds, maybe thousands, of people who now know your name, your values, and your voice. It means you pulled issues into the spotlight that no one else was talking about. It means you showed the next woman it was possible.

And here's the part that might surprise you: **People were watching.** Not just voters. Not just reporters. Future candidates. Students. Community members. Quiet donors. Fierce neighbors. Kids. Mentors. The next version of *you*.

You might never know the person who decided to speak up at work because they saw you speak out on a debate stage. You might never meet the girl who realized she could run someday because she saw your sign in her neighbor's yard. You might not see the ripple, but it's moving.

Losing doesn't erase any of that. In fact, it's often what *cements* your impact. Because when you lose and still show up? Still serve? Still support others, or try again, or speak out, or mentor the next one?

That's leadership. That's resilience in action. That's how movements get built, not in straight lines, but in spirals.

You're allowed to grieve. You're allowed to cry, rage, question everything, eat an entire pie alone, and disappear for a while. You're allowed to feel the loss *deeply* because it mattered.

And then?

You come back to yourself. You breathe. You look at what you built, because you *did* build something. A movement, a message, a new presence in your community's collective mind.

You made people listen. You made people *feel* again. You made the system a little less certain of itself, and a little more aware of what's coming.

And what's coming still might be you. Maybe in a different race. Maybe in a different role. Maybe not in elected office at all, but in something that emerged from the campaign, something that only revealed itself because you dared to say yes in the first place.

That's the thing about stepping into the arena: You never come out the same.

You come out with sharper instincts, deeper roots, a bigger network, and a clearer sense of what kind of leader you are.

You may have lost the race. But you didn't lose your voice. You didn't lose your community. And you sure as hell didn't lose your power.

This wasn't a detour. It was the road.

> And it's still unfolding—one brave, bold, unbecoming-the-old-you step at a time.

10

LIFE, AND LIFE AFTER OFFICE

> "At my age, in this still hierarchical time, people often ask me if I'm "passing the torch." I explain that I'm keeping my torch, thank you very much-and I'm using it to light the torches of others."
> — Gloria Steinem

You didn't pick up this book because you were bored. You picked it up because something in you was already burning.

Maybe it was rage.

Maybe it was love.

Maybe it was the stubborn, beautiful belief that things could be better.

Whatever it was, it led you here.

To a book that doesn't promise you power, but reminds you you already have it. To a voice that doesn't try to sell you a dream, but hands you the blueprint to build your own. To a message that's not about becoming someone else, but finally becoming *fully* yourself, in public, on purpose, and without apology.

Whether you won your race, served your term, lost by forty-seven votes, or chose not to run again, at some point, the campaign ends. The title changes. The calls slow down. The calendar opens up.

And there you are: no longer a candidate. Maybe no longer in office. Just…you.

And maybe for a moment, that feels disorienting. Who are you when you're not knocking doors, giving interviews, drafting policy, answering constituent emails at 10:43 p.m.?

Who are you when the adrenaline fades and the silence comes in?

Let me tell you, you are not done.

You are not "used up" or "former."

You are *seasoned*.

You are rooted.

You are full of wisdom, relationships, clarity, and momentum.

You've done what few people ever do, you've held power with integrity. And that doesn't disappear when your term ends. It deepens.

Because this? This is where legacy starts.

There is a whole world waiting for you on the other side of elected office.

You might step into consulting, bringing everything you learned on the ground to the candidates just getting started. You might become the mentor you *wish* you had. You might start a nonprofit, write a book, launch a podcast, or build something completely new from the questions that followed you through your term. You

Life, and Life After Office

might run again for something bigger, or something different, or something closer to home.

Or maybe, for the first time in a long time, you pause. You rest. You reset. You reclaim parts of yourself that got left behind in the campaign blur.

And then, when you're ready, you start to imagine: What do I want to build now that I know exactly who I am?

Because once you've held office, once you've worked inside the system, you're no longer guessing how change happens. You *know*.

And that kind of knowing makes you dangerous in the best way. It makes you powerful in rooms that used to intimidate you. It makes you magnetic to people looking for real leadership, not just polished soundbites. It makes you *irreplaceable* to movements that are rising right now and need someone just like you.

You're not stepping down.

You're stepping forward.

Here's the truth that most systems hope you never realize: You don't stop being powerful when you leave office, you become even more dangerous to the status quo, because now you know how the inside works *and* you're no longer bound by it.

That's legacy.

Not the kind that gets etched in plaques or recited at banquets. The kind that lives in neighborhoods, movements, and minds. The kind that outlasts the title and outgrows the job description. Because real legacy isn't about being remembered, it's about what you made possible for other people while you were here.

And now that you've held power with your whole heart, your voice, your fire, now that you've governed with a spine and made change with your own two hands, you get to carry that experience wherever you go next.

You get to be the woman in the room who already *did* the thing. You get to sit at the back of a candidate forum and smile quietly when a younger version of you takes the mic. You get to write, teach, organize, disrupt, nurture, advise, or just *be*, without explaining yourself.

You're not starting over. You're building further. Because your story isn't about holding office. It's about holding power with purpose, and then sharing it like wildfire.

There is no finish line.

Not in this work. Not in leadership. Not in the transformation of a country built on inequality and still trying to pretend it's fair.

You will rise, run, rise again.

You will lead, lose, love, rebuild, rage, and renew. You will watch the systems bend and unbend. You will watch people disappoint you, and then surprise you, and then show up in ways that leave you breathless. And through it all, you'll become someone you never imagined when this journey began.

Someone sharper. Softer. Bigger. Someone who doesn't wait to be asked. Someone who doesn't flinch when the pressure rises. Someone who knows exactly who she is, and what she's capable of, even when the room goes quiet.

This is who you are now. And this is only the beginning. Not because the seat was the goal, but because *you were always the point*.

You are not doing this alone. You are part of something bigger.

You are part of a wave of women who are done waiting. Who are tired of watching decisions get made without them. Who are stepping forward—not because it's easy, but because it's *time*. Some are running now. Some are still whispering the idea to themselves in the quiet of their car. Some are already sitting in office, holding it down with grace and grit, looking around and saying, *Where are the rest of us?*

You are the rest of us. You, in your fullness. You, in your clarity. You, rising again and again.

This isn't a book about how to get elected. It's a book about remembering who you are, and what happens when women start acting like they belong everywhere decisions are being made.

And whether your first race is still years away, or your campaign is already underway, or you've just closed one chapter and are preparing for whatever's next, you are now part of this lineage. This movement. This *shift*.

So rise. Run if it's right. Speak if you're called. And when it's time? Repeat. Lead in the way only you can. And if you ever forget who you are or what you're capable of, come back to this. Because this isn't a one-woman mission. It's a long, gorgeous, often messy, inheritance we're building together. And one day, a woman you've never met will run her race with a little more courage, a little more fire, a little more *freedom*—because of what you dared to do.

This is how we build it.
From the ground up.
Together.

AFTERWORD

HOW WILL WE KNOW IF ANY OF THIS MAKES A REAL DIFFERENCE?

So what if we're successful?

What happens if hundreds, thousands, of women run for office across the country, and a whole lot of them win? What happens when school boards, city councils, county commissions, statehouses, and eventually Congress are filled with women who lead with courage, compassion, and community-minded clarity?

The answer is: *everything begins to change.*

When women hold office in critical mass, research shows that **policy priorities shift**. Budgets are more likely to reflect the needs of families, children, healthcare, education, environmental stewardship, and social justice. But this isn't just about the top-line stats. This is about the **bottom-line impact** on our everyday lives.

You might be wondering—what would it actually take to tip the scales?

Political scientists and movement theorists frequently discuss the concept of **critical mass**, which refers to the point at which a sufficient number of people participate in a movement or system to create self-sustaining change. In political leadership, that tipping point is commonly estimated to be **30% representation** across key decision-making bodies.

So, what would that look like in practical terms?

If we do the math, there are over **500,000 elected offices** in the United States, the majority of which are at the local and state levels. That means we'd need **at least 150,000 women**, specifically women with community-first values, social equity in mind, and forward-thinking agendas, to hold office at every level to reach that tipping point.

Today, women make up roughly **32% of state legislatures**; however, their representation is far lower in many city councils, commissions, sheriff and judge races, and utility boards, *especially* in rural and low-income areas. And as Jessica Piper of Missouri will tell you, she doesn't even have a democrat or progressive on her ticket to vote for; she has no options. **Only about 23% of mayors** in cities with populations over 30,000 are women, and this number drops further for women of color, despite the good efforts of organizations like the National Association of Latino Elected and Appointed Officials (NALEO) and the National Black Caucus of State Legislators (NBCSL).

When those numbers rise, the culture of leadership changes. And it's not just about holding office; it's about governing differently. We'll know it's working when the numbers begin to shift, but more importantly, when lives begin to shift.

When a school district on the verge of collapse suddenly finds its classrooms funded, its teachers supported, and its children thriving, not because of a federal rescue, but because a woman on the school board fought for it like her own kid was in the room.

We'll know it's working when city council budgets begin to reflect what communities *actually* need: access to healthcare, food, clean water, and safety—not just in theory, but on every block.

Afterword

We'll know it's working when maternal and reproductive care is expanded and protected, not debated, not restricted, not used as a bargaining chip, but treated as sacred. Because women who've been there, who understand the stakes, are finally the ones holding the pen.

We'll know it's working when gun safety laws begin to reflect our lived reality. When we are no longer waiting for the next tragedy, but acting on the last one. When public safety means prevention, education, and care, not fear, profit, and paralysis.

We'll know it's working when infrastructure isn't just patched, it's reimagined, when policies reflect a long-term vision, not just political survival. When roads, power grids, and parks are designed for our grandchildren, not just for next quarter's report.

We'll know it's working when the rules apply to everyone, when campaign ethics and transparency are no longer optional, but expected. When doing the right thing isn't brave, it's standard.

We'll know it's working when people show up to vote, not just every four years, but in every election, because they feel seen, represented, and powerful.

And we'll really know it's working when…

A child in rural Arkansas and a single mother in Chicago both benefit from policies rooted in shared values and relentless compassion.

When elected, women not only do the work but *lift each other up*, coaching, mentoring, and insisting the door stay open behind them.

When the question, *"Where are the women?"* becomes laughably outdated, because everywhere decisions are being made, women are at the table. Not one. Not two. But enough.

Enough to tip the scales.

Enough to turn the tide.

Enough to save democracy.

At some point, when enough women step into leadership with ethics and empathy at the forefront, we will look back and realize *that was the turning point*. That was when the tides turned. That was when the heart of democracy started to beat stronger again.

We will know it's working not just by the laws that pass, but by the **lives that improve.**

So, if you ran, thank you.

If you're running, *let's go*.

And if you helped someone else rise into power, you're part of the revolution, too.

We're rebuilding what leadership looks like. And it's working.

So yes, this is about one seat, one race, one candidate at a time.

However, it's also about **the millions of lives that will be impacted** when we reach critical mass.

PART TWO

LET'S GET TO WORK

This is the part where I hand you a map and kiss you goodbye.

Okay, not quite—but I *am* the kind of person who likes to cut to the chase. I want to give you as many answers as possible to the questions you'll have at the start, and point you toward the right places to figure out the rest.

Here, you'll choose the seat you want to run for, and learn about the two tracks you'll need to study to run your race well: *you* as a candidate, and your *campaign* as an organized force.

To get you going, I've pulled together a **Candidate Starter Kit**, complete with a week-by-week checklist of tasks and milestones, a curated resource list featuring some of the best support out there for new candidates, and two glossaries, one for campaign lingo and another for government terms, so you don't have to Google every acronym on the fly.

This section gives you a light but sturdy framework to start building your unique run for office, because I couldn't fire you up to run and then leave you empty-handed.

So—what seat will it be?

Before you answer, take a good look around. What's *really* happening in your local elections?

You might be surprised by what you find. Maybe it's a school board with one voice dominating the room. Maybe it's a city council seat that's been uncontested for years. Maybe it's a parks commission that controls millions in public funds, but no one seems to be watching.

Digging into your local government is like pulling back a curtain. Suddenly, the vague frustration you've felt about "how things work" starts to come into focus. You'll see who's been making decisions, who's been missing from the table, and most importantly, where your voice could make a powerful difference.

This is where your run begins, not with a headline or a podium, but with curiosity. With questions. With a willingness to look closely and say, "I could do that, and I'd do it differently."

You should know:

More than 32% of local races across the U.S. go uncontested.

That means one person runs. One person wins. Every time. No competition. No accountability.

In some states, over 100 local offices go unfilled every year.

Yes—empty. No one files. The seat stays vacant. Or worse, it's quietly appointed without community input.

These races often happen off-cycle and under the radar.

Many voters don't even know they're happening. Turnout is low. Decisions get made anyway.

Most of these seats affect daily life more than the presidency ever will.

Let's Get to Work

City planning. Public safety. School funding. Property taxes. Library access. Small business support. Reproductive rights enforcement. You name it.

These are not unreachable positions.

Some are part-time. Some are volunteer. Many require only a few hundred votes, or fewer. And most have never had a woman like you run.

The following list covers most of the elected positions that affect our daily lives, from who picks your children's library books to who decides where your roads will go, how your taxes are calculated, and who enforces our laws. It's proof that **power doesn't just sit in DC**. It lives in all these seats, and every one of them matters.

Local (Municipal & County) Offices

Mayor

City Council / Board of Aldermen / Board of Trustees

County Commission / Board of Supervisors

City or County Clerk

Treasurer (City or County)

Assessor / Tax Assessor

Auditor or Comptroller (municipal)

Sheriff

District Attorney / Prosecuting Attorney

Coroner / Medical Examiner

City or County Attorney

City or County Auditor (Fiscal Oversight)

School Board Members

Water District Board Members

Planning & Zoning Commission

Public Utility District or Sewer Board Members

Fire District Board Members

Special District or Commission roles (e.g., Library Board, Parks & Rec, Transit Authority)

Local Judges / Justices of the Peace (Municipal, Probate, or Traffic Court)

Statewide Executive Offices

Governor

Lieutenant Governor

Attorney General

Secretary of State

State Treasurer

State Auditor or Comptroller

Superintendent of Public Instruction / Education

Insurance Commissioner

Agriculture Commissioner

Labor Commissioner

Land Commissioner

Other state regulatory officers (e.g., Mining Inspector, Public Utilities Commissioner)

State Legislative Offices

State Senator

State Representative / Assembly Member

State Comptroller or Legislative Budget Officer (in some states)

Other Elected Roles (Varies by Area)

Local judges (Superior, Circuit, District)

Prosecuting Attorneys (at county level)

Public Defenders (in some jurisdictions)

Constables or Marshals (town or county law enforcement)

Recorder of Deeds / Registrar of Titles

Clerk of Courts

Board of Equalization Members (some states)

County or Regional Health Board Members

How to Research Local Elections and Offices

If you're anything like most people, you were probably never taught how to research your local government. But if you're thinking about running—or even just becoming more engaged—you need to know who holds power in your community, what seats are open, and how often they change hands.

It's not as hard as it sounds. In fact, it's like unlocking a new layer of your hometown. Here's how to start:

1. Go to the Source

Every state has an official election authority, usually the Secretary of State's office or a State Board of Elections. That's where you'll find filing deadlines, rules for candidacy, upcoming election dates, and often a list of which offices are on the ballot this year.

2. Dig into County and City Resources

The state site is the overview, but your real action is local. Go to your county or city clerk's website (or office!) to find specific information about school boards, city councils, special districts, and more. These local sites often post past election results, current officeholders, and guidelines for how to file to run.

3. Find Out What's Actually on the Ballot

Want to see what voters in your area will be voting on this year? Look for a sample ballot or voter guide. Many counties release these online or by mail as the election nears. These documents are gold, they tell you what seats are up for grabs and what measures are being voted on.

4. Call and Ask

If you can't find something online, don't get discouraged. Call your county election office. Ask them, "Where can I find out what local offices are up for election this year?" or "Who do I contact if I want to file to run?" The folks answering the phones are usually very helpful—they want you to participate.

5. Look Beyond the Big Seats

Most people only think about mayors or city council members. But your local ballot might also include people who decide things like school curriculum, housing development, water management, or public safety funding. These lesser-known offices often go uncontested, or completely unfilled, because people don't realize they exist. That's your opening.

6. Get a Bird's Eye View of the Calendar

Local elections don't just happen every four years, they happen constantly. Cities and counties might hold elections every year, sometimes even more than once a year. Some are on the same schedule as federal elections, others are on their own calendar. Start tracking your area's election cycle so you know what's coming and when.

7. Map the Landscape

As you research, keep a running list of:

- Who currently holds each seat
- When their term ends
- What the district boundaries are
- How many people vote in those races
- Which ones are elected vs. appointed

This will give you a clear sense of where you could run, and where you could win.

You might think the president or Congress runs the show, but it's your city council that sets your zoning laws. It's your school board that shapes the next generation. It's your utility district that determines who gets clean water.

Understanding who's in charge where you live, how they got there, and when their seat is up for grabs puts power back in your hands.

The truth is, the political machine counts on you not knowing. But you're not going to sit this one out. You're going to learn. You're going to look closer. And pretty soon, you're going to realize: not only is this not as confusing as it seemed, it's absolutely doable.

And maybe, just maybe, that empty seat no one's talking about?

It's got your name on it.

YOU SAID YES?!

*S*o, you said it out loud. Or maybe you whispered it into the mirror.

I'm running.

Whether you've filed the paperwork, launched your announcement, or are still steadying your nerves from the weight of the decision, you've crossed a threshold. You're not on the sidelines anymore. You're in it.

Let's be clear: this is no small thing.

Declaring your candidacy means you're offering yourself up to be a voice for your community. You're choosing to enter an arena that is often loud, messy, and unpredictable, not because it's easy, but because you care. That matters.

So take a breath. Feel the ground under your feet. Then let's talk about what comes next.

You're Officially a Candidate—Now What?

Running for office is a dual journey:

You're building yourself as a candidate.

And you're building the campaign that will carry your name into the hearts and minds of voters.

Building Yourself as a Candidate

This is the inner work.

It's the part no one sees but everyone feels when you speak.

You'll need to get *crystal clear* on why you're running. Not the surface-level talking points, but the fire-in-your-belly reasons. What brought you here? What breaks your heart? What are you determined to fix?

Then, you'll want to identify what makes you the one for the job, your unique skills, your lived experience, your values, and how you lead. Think about how to express those things in your voice, your story, and yes, your look. From your website photos to your social media presence to the way you introduce yourself at the farmers market, you're shaping an image of leadership that's grounded in truth.

But even the most authentic message can be drowned out if it's delivered without confidence. This is where you begin to hone your public speaking. You learn to speak clearly, concisely, and powerfully, whether you're at a kitchen table or on a stage.

You'll also want to understand the core principles of campaign ethics, compliance, and transparency, not because you plan to mess up, but because you don't want to. This work is about staying in integrity *and* staying in the race.

And yes, you'll need to get comfortable being visible. That includes media interviews, community forums, maybe even debates. You don't have to do this perfectly. But you do need to be present and prepared.

You don't have to figure it all out alone. There are trusted resources that will walk with you every step of the way:

- Candidate School (highly recommended), learn everything you need to know about running for office in a 20 day online course.
- Vote Run Lead, She Should Run, Ignite National—visit these websites for dynamic resources.
- Mentorship and coaching from women who've run before (especially in your community), and who still believe in the next generation of leaders (that's you).

Building Your Campaign

If the first part is soul work, this part is systems work.

Campaigns aren't just passionate ideas, they're operations. And every operation needs a plan.

Start with your team.

Who do you trust to be in your corner, to offer sound advice, honest feedback, and maybe hold your phone while you knock on doors? You don't need a massive staff. You need a few sharp, loyal people who believe in your vision.

Next: fundraising.

Every campaign costs money. The question isn't *can* you raise it—it's *how* will you? Get clear on your budget. Understand what you need, what's realistic, and where to start. Remember: donors don't just give to issues. They give to people. Make it personal.

Then: communications.

How will people hear about you? Is your website live? Do your social media platforms reflect your voice? What do your flyers and yard signs say before you even open your mouth? These things matter more than you think, they speak for you when you're not in the room.

And of course: voter outreach.

You're not just running to talk. You're running to win votes. That means a ground game. It means mailers, phone calls, door-knocking, community events, GOTV (Get Out The Vote) plans. It means organizing in a way that makes people *feel* something. Because people vote when they feel seen.

The Heart of It

Whether you're launching a scrappy grassroots campaign with five volunteers and a folding table, or you're entering a high-stakes citywide race, know this:

Your clarity will attract people.

Your consistency will build trust.

And your connection to your community will carry you farther than any perfect campaign strategy ever could.

This is your moment.

You've said yes.

Now, we build.

CAMPAIGN STARTER KIT

Your first 90 days as a candidate, mapped and manageable.

You did it. You made the decision to run. Maybe it was a moment of rage, maybe it was a whisper that wouldn't go away, or maybe it was a steady, growing fire inside you that said, "Now is the time." However you got here, welcome.

You are not expected to know everything from day one. No one does. Campaigns are built from the ground up, just like movements, just like change. What you bring, your voice, your lived experience, your integrity, is the foundation your campaign will stand on. The rest you'll learn, build, and refine with time.

This starter kit is here to walk with you through the first three months. Month by month, task by task, this is your invitation to take meaningful, strategic action without burning out or losing yourself. Because I don't just want you to get elected. I want you to thrive as you do it.

Campaign Systems Setup: Your First 30 Days

Week 1–2: Lay the Foundation

Get Your Candidate Essentials in Order

- Secure your EIN (Employer Identification Number)
- Open a dedicated campaign bank account
- File your candidate paperwork with the appropriate election office
- Read your local and state campaign finance laws (yes, all of them—take notes!)
- Decide whether to run as a party-affiliated or nonpartisan candidate
- Sign up for the *Ready to Run Newsletter*—it's aims to prep candidates, is focused on women and it's FREE

Start Building Your Brand & Messaging

- Clarify your "Why I'm Running" statement
- Write your bio and collect any professional headshots
- Identify your core campaign values and three to five issue priorities
- Begin working with a designer or agency to create your campaign logo, colors, and typography
- Purchase your domain and build a simple campaign website with a donations button and email sign-up

Get Visible (Digitally)

- Create your campaign email address
- Set up your social media accounts (start with Facebook, Instagram, and/or X/Twitter)
- Create a Linktree (or equivalent) for social bios

Campaign Starter Kit

Week 3–4: Activate Your Voter & Volunteer Engine

Secure & Organize Your Voter Data

- Contact your local or state party or election board to access your voter file
- Import it into your preferred tool (NationBuilder, VAN, or Airtable/Google Sheets)
- Identify key data points: voting frequency, party affiliation, age, location
- Segment voters by precinct or region and begin building outreach lists

Set Up Your Core Systems

- Choose and configure your outreach tools VAN/MiniVan, Reach, Civitech, or Airtable)
- Choose your email platform (Mailchimp, ActionNetwork, or Constant Contact)
- Connect donation tracking (ActBlue, Anedot, or NationBuilder)
- Start a contact log: record conversations, yard sign requests, donations, and volunteer interest

Start Assembling Your Team

- Identify or recruit a campaign treasurer (compliance + donations)
- Appoint or consider a campaign manager or lead volunteer
- Begin creating a list of trusted advisors or mentors
- Ask for an early endorsement from a local or state elected official

Build Early Momentum

- Announce your candidacy via email and social media
- Schedule your first house party or launch event
- Begin gathering email addresses and phone numbers from supporters
- Draft your first outreach script for door knocking, texting, or phone banking

Campaign Starter Kit

The Next 60 Days: Grow, Organize, and Mobilize

Weeks 5–8: Start Building Power

Deepen Your Message + Materials

- Finalize your campaign's core messaging: your story, your platform, your promises
- Write and practice a compelling stump speech
- Draft FAQ responses and talking points for hot-button issues
- Order campaign materials: yard signs, palm cards, door hangers, banners
- Finalize your campaign brand kit: colors, fonts, photography, logo usage
- Develop a signature look for social media graphics and print pieces

Expand Your Digital Reach

- Build a content calendar for social media
- Schedule regular email updates to supporters (every two to three weeks minimum)
- Launch a "Meet the Candidate" video or introductory reel
- Begin tracking basic engagement metrics (open rates, clicks, shares, comment)
- Set up Google Analytics and Meta Pixel on your website for deeper data insights

Host Events & Listen

- Host at least two meet-and-greets, town halls, or community forums
- Speak at local clubs, neighborhood associations, or civic group meetings

- Create a "listening tour" approach. Take notes on community priorities and questions
- Practice answering questions clearly and calmly in front of groups
- Begin building relationships with local reporters and influencers

Weeks 9–12: Mobilize Your People

Build a Volunteer Base

- Create a volunteer sign-up form (on your site and social media)
- Start calling/texting supporters to ask how they'd like to help
- Assign clear roles: social media help, data entry, canvassing, phone banking
- Schedule volunteer trainings (online or in-person)
- Create a private Facebook group or Slack channel to keep volunteers informed and motivated

Start Field Work (Outreach!)

- Cut turf (target walk lists) using your voter data system
- Knock on doors or phonebank weekly. Track all conversations
- Prioritize high-turnout precincts and known supporters
- Log every contact: voter ID, level of support, follow-up needed
- Order clipboards, walk sheets, volunteer name badges, and literature bags

Step Up Fundraising

- Set a clear monthly fundraising goal
- Hold a small-dollar fundraising event
- Send targeted fundraising emails (with urgency and story-based ask)
- Follow up personally with twenty-five top prospective donors
- Thank every donor with a note, email, or call

Build Endorsements & Relationships

- Reach out to past elected officials, respected community leaders, and aligned orgs
- Submit questionnaires to local political clubs and civic organizations
- Collect testimonials from supporters and allies
- Begin planning for earned media (letters to the editor, op-eds, local podcast interviews)

Key Milestone by Day Ninty:

You should now have...

- A recognizable candidate brand
- A functioning and active campaign website and social media presence
- A base of volunteers who are trained and activated
- A growing voter contact list
- A donor list with momentum
- A presence in your community that people are starting to talk about

Running Resources

Print, Branding & Signage

Local Sign Printers
Most local print shops offer custom yard signs, banners, and mailers with quick turnaround times. Be sure to ask whether they have experience working on political campaigns, or get referrals from candidates who regularly run in your area.

Online Printing Options
Search "campaign sign printing" online to find the latest deals. Offers change frequently, and Google typically surfaces the most competitive and campaign-ready providers first.

Merchandise
For union-made campaign swag, Bright Blue Ink in Austin, Texas, is a trusted provider of quality items.

Electa
Electa is a branding agency that helps women candidates build clear, powerful brands by aligning their voice, vision, and visuals. Your website, print materials, and social media should all work together to earn votes—Electa makes that happen. (Full disclosure: I own it.)
Website: electaagency.com

Data & Analytics

Aristotle
Aristotle offers comprehensive tools for voter data, compliance, and campaign management—handy for state and local campaigns.

Election Data Services, Inc.
This organization specializes in redistricting support, census data, and voter turnout analytics.
Website: electiondataservices.com

GoodParty.org
Good Party empowers independent and underdog candidates with personalized voter data, AI-powered outreach tools, strategic planning, and advisory support.

NGP VAN
NGP VAN provides fundraising, compliance, and donor management software trusted by many progressive campaigns.

Civitech
Civitech offers creative solutions for targeted voter registration and campaign tools like the Running Mate app, designed for voter outreach and data management at various campaign levels.

FollowTheMoney.org
This nonprofit provides transparency by tracking state and local campaign contributions and independent expenditures.

Party.Org
Party.org is building a new, non-ideological political party with the infrastructure and support to field candidates across the spectrum.

Candidate Training & Skilling

She Should Run
A nonpartisan nonprofit that encourages and supports women who are considering running for office.

Vote Run Lead
Provides expert training to help women win state and local races with confidence and impact.

Candidate School
Candidate School helps women become grounded, skillful, and informed candidates through high-level, accessible coursework and optional coaching.
Website: dianamaldonado.com (I'm affiliated with this program.)

Run for Something
This national organization inspires, educates, and endorses progressive candidates—especially young and first-time office seekers.

Ready to Run Newsletter
A free weekly newsletter packed with lessons, strategy, and tools to help women run and win.
Website: ReadytoRunNow.com (I also work here.)

Emerge America
Emerge recruits and trains Democratic women to run for office at all levels of government.

EMILY's List / Run to Win
Focused on electing pro-choice Democratic women, this organization offers support with fundraising, endorsements, and campaign strategy.

Annie's List (Texas)
This Texas-based PAC provides training, funding, and endorsements for progressive women running for office.

Campaign Starter Kit

National Women's Political Caucus (NWPC)
This grassroots, multi-partisan organization offers candidate support and training across the country.

Public Leadership Education Network (PLEN)
PLEN provides leadership and public policy seminars for college-aged women interested in public service.

New American Leaders
New American Leaders offers training and support specifically for first- and second-generation Americans, especially immigrant women, seeking elected office.

Campaigns & Elections
Their website includes a "Consultant Directory" under the Resources tab, making it easy to find political professionals.

AAPC, American Association of Political Consultants
The AAPC site includes a "Find a Consultant" tool to help you locate experts in campaign strategy and media.

Campaign Finance, Fundraising & Compliance

Federal Election Commission (FEC)
The FEC provides rules, regulations, contribution limits, and reporting requirements for federal candidates.

FollowTheMoney.org
A go-to source for transparency in state-level political giving, offering insight into contributors, trends, and influence.

Political Consulting & Advertising

Political Marketing Agencies like Reach Voters, These agencies offer a full range of campaign services, including messaging, digital advertising, and field strategy.

Top Consulting Firms
These full-service firms specialize in large-scale media production, campaign operations, and strategic consulting. While often beyond the budget of small races, they're worth keeping on your radar as your political career grows.

Digital Tools & Election Security

CISA (Cybersecurity & Infrastructure Security Agency)
CISA offers trusted resources for securing campaign websites, voter data, and digital infrastructure from cyber threats.

VAN (Voter Activation Network)
This essential tool helps campaigns manage canvassing, phone-banking, and voter contact—integrated with party data and optimized for team use.

MiniVAN
The mobile version of VAN, MiniVAN allows volunteers to knock on doors, collect voter info, and track results from their phone or tablet.

Reach
Reach is a relational organizing app that helps your supporters connect with friends and family who may be potential voters.

NationBuilder
This platform integrates website building, email marketing, and voter data to help candidates manage volunteers, donors, and events.

ActBlue
ActBlue is a trusted donation platform that simplifies fundraising and makes it easy for supporters to contribute online.

Google Sheets or Airtable
These low-cost (or free) tools are ideal for tracking volunteer shifts, donations, outreach, and more. Airtable includes helpful automations and customizable layouts.

Mailchimp or Constant Contact
Use these platforms to send campaign emails, organize your contacts by location or interest, and schedule regular communications.

Print it out and make it your own plan!

Would you like to download the Campaign Starter Kit + receive bonus materials to help you launch your campaign?

Scan here:

GLOSSARY OF CAMPAIGN TERMS

Canvassing
Definition: The act of going door-to-door or person-to-person to talk with voters and promote a candidate or issue.
Example: Volunteers spent the weekend canvassing neighborhoods ahead of the election.
When It Comes Up: During voter outreach efforts, especially in local campaigns.

GOTV (Get Out The Vote)
Definition: Efforts aimed at encouraging people to vote, especially in the final days of a campaign.
Example: The campaign launched a massive GOTV push the weekend before Election Day.
When It Comes Up: In the final weeks or days of an election cycle.

Field Operations
Definition: The portion of a campaign focused on direct voter contact like canvassing, phone banking, and events.
Example: The field operations team organized canvassing routes and volunteer shifts.
When It Comes Up: Throughout the campaign, particularly in grassroots efforts.

Polling
Definition: The process of surveying public opinion to gather data about voters' preferences.
Example: Polling showed the candidate gaining support among younger voters.
When It Comes Up: During campaign strategy, messaging decisions, and media planning.

Fundraising
Definition: The act of collecting money to support a political campaign.
Example: Fundraising events helped the candidate meet quarterly financial goals.
When It Comes Up: Early in the campaign and throughout the election cycle.

War Chest
Definition: Funds that a candidate has accumulated for campaign use.
Example: With a solid war chest, the candidate was able to launch ads earlier than expected.
When It Comes Up: When evaluating campaign strength and strategic options.

Glossary of Campaign Terms

Opposition Research
Definition: Investigating an opponent's record, policies, or personal background.
Example: The team uncovered inconsistencies in the incumbent's voting record during opposition research.
When It Comes Up: When preparing debates, speeches, or targeted messaging.

Endorsement
Definition: Public support for a candidate from a person, organization, or publication.
Example: The union's endorsement gave the campaign a major credibility boost.
When It Comes Up: When building legitimacy and support networks.

Ballot Access
Definition: The process and requirements for getting a candidate's name on the ballot.
Example: She gathered signatures to meet ballot access requirements in her district.
When It Comes Up: Early in the campaign during filing and petition deadlines.

Stump Speech
Definition: A candidate's standard campaign speech used at most events and rallies.
Example: He delivered his stump speech with a few local references added for the crowd.
When It Comes Up: At campaign events, debates, and media appearances.

Compliance
Definition: The act of adhering to legal regulations regarding campaign finance, advertising, and disclosures.
Example: The treasurer ensured all donations were recorded properly for FEC compliance.
When It Comes Up: Throughout the campaign, especially with donations and reporting.

Ethics
Definition: Standards that govern appropriate conduct for candidates, campaign staff, and public officials.
Example: She recused herself from voting due to an ethics concern involving a family business.
When It Comes Up: When dealing with conflicts of interest, transparency, or public accountability.

Disclosure
Definition: The legal requirement to publicly report contributions, expenditures, and affiliations.
Example: All major donations must be listed in the campaign's disclosure report.
When It Comes Up: Regularly during campaign finance reporting periods.

In-Kind Contribution
Definition: A non-monetary donation, such as free office space, design work, or supplies.
Example: The donated event venue was reported as an in-kind contribution.
When It Comes Up: During budgeting, compliance reviews, and donation tracking.

Glossary of Campaign Terms

Filing Deadline
Definition: The last date by which a candidate must submit paperwork to appear on the ballot.
Example: She rushed to gather signatures ahead of the filing deadline.
When It Comes Up: Early in the campaign—critical for eligibility.

Treasurer
Definition: The campaign official responsible for managing finances, compliance, and reporting.
Example: The treasurer filed the quarterly campaign finance report on time.
When It Comes Up: Throughout the campaign, especially in fundraising and spending oversight.

Glossary of Local and State Government Terms

Ordinance
Definition: A law or regulation enacted by a city or county government.
Example: The city council passed an ordinance banning single-use plastic bags.
When It Comes Up: During legislative sessions, policy proposals, city council meetings.

Resolution
Definition: A formal expression of opinion or intention voted by an official body.
Example: The county commission adopted a resolution declaring a housing crisis.
When It Comes Up: To express values, set intent, or take a stance without passing a law.

Quorum
Definition: The minimum number of members required to conduct official business.
Example: The board meeting couldn't proceed because they didn't have a quorum.
When It Comes Up: At any official meeting that requires a vote or decision-making.

Charter
Definition: A legal document establishing a municipality and defining its powers.
Example: The city is governed by a charter that allows for a strong-mayor system.
When It Comes Up: When incorporating a city or changing local government structure.

Levy
Definition: To impose or collect a tax by authority.
Example: The school board voted to levy a property tax increase for education funding.
When It Comes Up: In budget processes and tax discussions.

Appropriation
Definition: A legislative grant of money for a specific purpose.
Example: The legislature passed an appropriation for road repairs across the state.
When It Comes Up: During state and local budgeting sessions.

Public Comment
Definition: Designated time for citizens to speak during a public meeting.
Example: During public comment, residents voiced concern over the zoning proposal.
When It Comes Up: At hearings, council meetings, school board sessions.

Glossary of Campaign Terms

Zoning
Definition: Regulations that govern land use and development within a municipality.
Example: The planning commission held a hearing on rezoning downtown for mixed-use.
When It Comes Up: In urban planning, housing, development, and business regulations.

Referendum
Definition: A direct vote in which the electorate decides on a specific proposal or law.
Example: Voters approved a referendum legalizing recreational cannabis.
When It Comes Up: When placing a measure directly on the ballot for public vote.

Constituent
Definition: A resident of a district or area represented by an elected official.
Example: The council member met with her constituents to discuss public safety concerns.
When It Comes Up: Anytime an official engages with the people they serve.

Amendment
Definition: A formal change or addition proposed or made to a bill, law, or constitution.
Example: The legislature passed an amendment to increase funding for rural schools.
When It Comes Up: During legislative sessions, constitutional reform, or ballot initiatives.

Caucus
Definition: A meeting of members of a political party or group to coordinate policy or select candidates.
Example: The Democratic caucus met to decide their legislative priorities for the session.
When It Comes Up: Party strategy, internal elections, legislative alignment.

Redistricting
Definition: The process of drawing new electoral district boundaries.
Example: Redistricting shifted voting boundaries and changed the makeup of the district.
When It Comes Up: After a census or during gerrymandering reform debates.

Gerrymandering
Definition: Manipulating electoral district boundaries for political advantage.
Example: The court ruled that the map was an example of racial gerrymandering.
When It Comes Up: Redistricting lawsuits, electoral fairness debates.

Home Rule
Definition: The power of a local city or county to self-govern independently from state laws.
Example: Because of home rule, the city passed stricter environmental ordinances.
When It Comes Up: Local governance authority and charter city powers.

Glossary of Campaign Terms

Sunshine Laws
Definition: Laws that require certain proceedings of government to be open or available to the public.
Example: Sunshine laws allowed reporters to request internal city communications.
When It Comes Up: Transparency, open records, press access to meetings.

Filibuster
Definition: A procedural tactic used to delay or block legislative action, often by extended debate.
Example: The senator launched a filibuster to block the voting rights bill.
When It Comes Up: State senates, high-stakes legislation, minority party tactics.

Whip
Definition: A party official responsible for ensuring members vote in line with party strategy.
Example: The majority whip counted votes before the education bill reached the floor.
When It Comes Up: Legislative vote planning, party leadership roles.

Veto
Definition: The power of an executive to reject a bill passed by the legislature.
Example: The governor vetoed the bill to restrict mail-in voting.
When It Comes Up: Governor or mayoral decisions, override attempts.

Recall Election
Definition: A process by which voters can remove an elected official before the end of their term.
Example: Citizens organized a recall election after widespread mismanagement.
When It Comes Up: Accountability, direct democracy tools, local crises.

This should give you a strong start. You've got the map, the resources, and the spark; now all that's left is to begin. You don't have to know everything right now; you just have to keep moving forward, one step at a time. And if you've been reading carefully, you already know where to find me if you have questions. I'm rooting for you—loudly, proudly, and without hesitation.

Thank you for reading this book. Truly. Thank you for opening your heart and mind to the possibility of public service, and for daring to believe that your voice matters. If you've decided to run for office, I am honored to have played even a small role in helping you take that first step. And if you've decided it's not your time or your path, thank you still, for carrying the message forward. Maybe you'll hand this book to someone who doesn't yet see themselves as a leader, but should. Maybe you'll tell a friend, a sister, a neighbor: "I see something in you."

That's how we grow this movement. That's how we build the kind of future that feels good to live in. I'll say it again, from the ground up. Together.

Glossary of Campaign Terms

Print it out and make it your own plan!
Would you like to download the Campaign Starter Kit + receive bonus materials to help you launch your campaign?
Scan here:

INDEX OF WORKS CITED

American Academy of Arts & Sciences. (2020). *Our Common Purpose: Reinventing American Democracy for the 21st Century.* https://www.amacad.org/ourcommonpurpose

Ballotpedia. (n.d.). *Local government in the United States.* https://ballotpedia.org/Local_government

Center for American Women and Politics (CAWP). (2023). *Women in Elective Office 2023.* Eagleton Institute of Politics, Rutgers University. https://cawp.rutgers.edu/

Collective PAC. (n.d.). *About Us.* https://collectivepac.org/

Emily's List. (n.d.). *Our Mission.* https://emilyslist.org

Fair Fight. (n.d.). *About.* https://fairfight.com/

Ignite National. (n.d.). *Building a movement of young women who are ready and eager to become the next generation of political leaders.* https://ignitenational.org

National Conference of State Legislatures (NCSL). (2023). *State Elections Legislation Database.* https://www.ncsl.org/elections-and-campaigns/elections-legislation-database

National League of Cities (NLC). (n.d.). *Cities 101 - Forms of Municipal Government.* https://www.nlc.org/resource/cities-101-forms-of-municipal-government/

National Women's Political Caucus. (n.d.). *About NWPC.* https://www.nwpc.org/

Ploughshares Fund. (n.d.). *Women, Peace, and Security.* https://ploughshares.org/women-peace-security

RepresentWomen. (n.d.). *Building a 21st Century Democracy with Gender Balance.* https://www.representwomen.org

Run for Something. (n.d.). *Recruiting and supporting young diverse progressives to run for down-ballot races.* https://runforsomething.net

She Should Run. (n.d.). *Inspiring women to run for office.* https://www.sheshouldrun.org

United Nations. (2000). *UN Security Council Resolution 1325 on Women, Peace and Security.* https://www.un.org/womenwatch/osagi/wps/

VoteRunLead. (n.d.). *Training barrier-breaking women to unleash their political power.* https://voterunlead.org

Women's Public Leadership Network (WPLN). (n.d.). *Educating, organizing, and inspiring center- and right-leaning women to seek public office.* https://womenspublicleadership.net

Women & Politics Institute, American University. (n.d.). *WeLead Program.* https://www.american.edu/spa/wpi/

Yale Program on Climate Change Communication. (2021). *Politics & Global Warming, April 2021.* https://climatecommunication.yale.edu/publications/politics-global-warming-april-2021/

ABOUT THE AUTHOR
CHRISTY JAYNES

Christy Jaynes is a three-time bestselling author, longtime coach, and a fearless champion of women stepping into public power. She's a collaborator and content creator for **Candidate School**, a transformational program that helps women prepare to run for office with clarity, strategy, and soul. She's also the founder of **Electa**, a modern political branding agency dedicated to helping candidates find their voice, claim their vision, and show up with unforgettable impact.

For more than a decade, Christy has coached women from all walks of life, entrepreneurs, artists, activists, and first-time candidates, guiding them through growth, transformation, and the kind of inner clarity that leads to outer change. Her work sits at the intersection of purpose, politics, and bold personal leadership.

She believes that women don't need permission to lead, they just need the right support. This book is part of that support.

Christy lives, creates, and occasionally rants about democracy in St. Louis, Missouri.

www.ingramcontent.com/pod-product-compliance
Lightning Source LLC
Chambersburg PA
CBHW020547030426
42337CB00013B/1003